Library Cat

Library Cat

The Observations of a Thinking Cat

Alex Howard

Illustrations by Miriam Wilson

BLACK & WHITE PUBLISHING

First published 2016
by Black & White Publishing Ltd
29 Ocean Drive, Edinburgh EH6 6JL

1 3 5 7 9 10 8 6 4 2   16 17 18 19

ISBN: 978 1 78530 016 5

Typeset by 3btype.com
Printed and bound by Pulsio SARL

To my parents and Ellie

Acknowledgements

To all the students who sent me pictures of Library Cat on Facebook. This book is for you. To Ellie – my girlfriend and de facto editor – for putting up with my neurotic doubts. To Fr. Lawrence Lew OP. for allowing me to use his wonderful pictures, and Fr. Dermot Morrin for allowing me to hijack the brain of his cat.

Also, I'd like to thank Penny Fielding, Jonathan Wild, Lee Spinks and James Loxley at the University of Edinburgh's department of English Literature for believing in my writing from early on. To writers Tracey S. Rosenberg and Alan Warner for your support and advice, and Sinéad Docherty for your valuable industry insight. And to my parents, for getting me to this point.

Thanks also to my illustrator Miriam Wilson and the exemplary team at Black & White Publishing; you couldn't have made a debut novelist feel more welcome!

And, of course, to Jordan – the real "Library Cat" – for allowing me so graciously to channel his thoughts.

Library Cat's Map

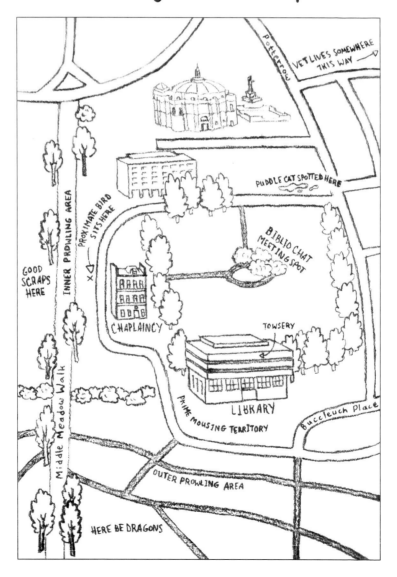

Library Cat's Brain

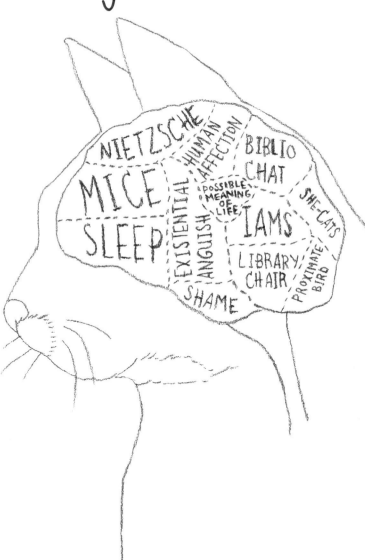

Contents

And those who were seen dancing
were thought to be insane by those
who could not hear the music.

Friedrich Nietzsche

Library Cat

Library Cat is not like most cats. This is because Library Cat is a thinking cat.

I think therefore I am, thought Library Cat one autumn morning. (You see what I mean?)

Library Cat lives in Edinburgh. He has one white paw and one black paw with a white tip that makes it look like it has been dipped into a churn of fresh milk. Along his back runs fur so fine and ethereal that in the correct light it shimmers like a cornfield in a summer breeze. His eyes are green and flecked with gold – more alert than a normal cat's. Just right of his nose is a little white splodge, as if his mouth had got too close while lapping from the same milk churn, and from this mouth extend whiskers so unusually elegant and curled that one might suspect, on seeing them alone, that there is something magical about Library Cat.

Library Cat was born eight years ago in the Edinburgh University Chaplaincy. Despite a rather biblical sense of self-importance, he is not, however, an especially religious cat. Among the litter, he has six other brothers and sisters. Library Cat is the only thinking cat among them. His brothers and sisters had gone on to live perfectly pleasant lives, with warm firesides and good cardboard boxes to sleep in, they were well-fed and well-groomed and they had become a most serviceable set of mouse catchers.

But things had turned out a little differently for Library Cat. This is because, a mere two months following his birth, something started to kindle inside his mind. It was the spark of thought. He therefore did what all thinking cats are destined to do: seek out books. This is why you can still find him in and out of Edinburgh University Library to this day, sitting in his favourite turquoise chair in the foyer, the perfect place in which to sleep, think and observe.

Library Cat has many things he likes, and many more things he dislikes. Among his favourite things are bacon rind, tickles behind the left ear, and the stunning eloquence of *The Complete Works of Friedrich Nietzsche*. Among his most disliked things are fireworks, water (except to drink), unsubstantiated claims, the Black Dog (from whom he lived in terror), noises between the frequency range of 4.5 and 16.5 hertz, Human-to-Animal condescension, the beige colour of pot-hole puddles, drug trafficking, cucumbers and exuberance.

Library Cat has a French cousin called Biblio Chat. Biblio Chat is also a thinking cat. This does not mean he and Library Cat agree on everything. Far from it. Biblio Chat detests bacon rind. It lacks, if we are to quote him accurately, *Le Crunch Facteur*.

Among Biblio Chat's most cherished things are radiators between the temperature range of 38 and 40.5 degrees centigrade, tickles under his neck, being combed and pâté. He too hates Human-to-Animal condescension as well the recent rise in political apathy. He is also more successful with girl cats than Library Cat.

Library Cat often found himself thinking negatively towards his cousin: *Damn him and his showy rejection of dried food! What's wrong with Whiskas Tuna? It's adequate nourishment, is it not? The Crunch Factor indeed!*

But Biblio Chat is a thinking cat, and that counts for a lot. There are precious few thinking cats on this earth. Indeed, a thinking cat is lucky if he finds one other thinking cat with whom to share thoughts during his entire lifetime, let alone one who is also a blood relation.

Library Cat does not own much, though one might be forgiven for believing that he owns everything he ever sat on, looked at, biffed with his paw and chased through the grass. But one thing Library Cat definitely does own are his thoughts. They twist through his mind like the threads of dye in water. Some are delicious and featured succulent mice, warm beds and the crisp, colourful imagery of Sylvia Plath; others – like paradoxes, quadratic equations and Human warfare – are grey and dead-ended, and strike tiny sparks of discord across his little feline synapses. One thing that he's sure about, however, is that his thoughts… all his thoughts… are his own. And nobody knows about them, not least of all any Human.

And what a relief that is, thought Library Cat.

So the time has come, Human, to sit back and behold those tiny white pearls of thought of a cat's mind. Read carefully; you never know, you might just learn something. After all, Library Cat thinks us Humans have it all wrong. And he's going to show us why...

Breakfast

…in which our hero eats things, and momentarily impersonates a policeman

Library Cat was trying to sleep. He was counting sheep to help him:

One, and indeed, Two, and indeed Three, and indeed, Four, and indeed, Fiv – hmm, would we call that one a "sheep"? Could be a goat?… And indeed Five, and indeed Six, and indeed Seven…

It was early morning. All around Library Cat's bed, dust sparkled in a thin ray of sunlight. Around him, books rested in hidden corners. There were thick books, small books, old books with golden spines and bookmarks of red ribbon, boxes of books, and – his favourite – books with small slivers of catnip sitting on top of them.

And indeed Eight, and indeed Nine, and indeed, Ten...
On the floor was more ribbon, this time chewed and frayed, and scattered like confetti. To one side was a scruffy bowl of dried food and water, and beyond it, a dusty cat flap that swayed gently in the gusty autumn air.

And indeed Eleven, and indeed Twel... OH IT'S NO USE!
Library Cat opened his eyes, a resigned expression on his face. Lazily he raised himself up on his four paws and arched his back up into an old medieval humpbacked bridge. He paused. Then, after a brief shake of the head, he yawned, revealing a whole line of pink, concertinaed ridges along the back of his mouth.

That feels most pleasing, he thought.

And now his paws. First the black one with the white tip – he stretched it right out like a policeman's truncheon raised in warning. Next, his white paw followed in slow succession. And then he rested (for too much sudden exercise is detrimental to a cat's constitution). Some moments later, after a brief snooze, he rose fully and walked over to the window. His bedroom was in the basement, and in order to see the outside world he was forced to leap upon a low windowsill and raise himself up on his hind legs, his forepaws on the windowpane, so that his eye line was just about level with the pavement outside. Today, he gazed out blearily. Beyond the cobblestoned road that lay a short trot from the chaplaincy's railings was George Square, littered with coloured leaves that spun in little vortices of wind along the pavement. It was early autumn and the light was apricot coloured, and as the little leaves spun crisply down the pavement, Library Cat sensed for the first time that summer was well and truly over.

A few moments later, Library Cat was pushing his head out of his grubby cat flap into the chilly morning air. All was perfectly still. A bolt of cold shivered through his paw as he touched it down upon the damp pavement stone. Around him, the tenements eyed each other like battalions of troops frozen in the anticipation of an impending battle. In the distance beyond the square, a bus lumbered drowsily through the early morning mist. On the air was the Weetabixy scent of the McEwan's brewery that was so characteristic of the city this time of year.

One must not think on an empty stomach, considered Library Cat, and with that he looked down at his paws. The gaps between the cobbles were rinded with dirt and moss, but deep within these gaps there lay little treats that only a cat's eye might see – bugs! After voraciously lapping up some creepy-crawly hors d'oeuvres, Library Cat turned right and headed to Edinburgh University's Main Library that stood like a cold grey cube in the silent morning air.

❖ Recommended Reading

Ulysses by James Joyce.

❖ Food consumed

1 x fat beetle, and 1 x millipede thing.

❖ Mood

Moderate, rising. Becoming good.

❖ Discovery about Humans

They don't come out in the early morning.

Freshers

...in which our hero visits the Towsery,
meets some Freshers, and refuses to find
the word "Bush" remotely amusing

Library Cat peered into the library and saw many things. For a non-thinking cat, it would have seemed a perilous place to be sure.

Firstly, there were sliding glass doors which, when closed, were the perfect width apart for cat decapitation. Then there was a staircase that zigzagged high up into the roof that reminded him of an Escher painting. At this early hour in the morning, the foyer was still quiet; only the television screens buzzed softly displaying their images of books and artefacts, while upon the ceiling a large projector hummed as it shone a dust-sparkled ray of light upon a white screen that bore the heading "Information for Students". To the right, there was a desk of Humans that looked important. On busier days, these Humans sounded a bell and barked in incandescent rage at every fourth or fifth Human attempting to leave, barring them from freedom and jabbing their fingers accusingly at the student Humans' rucksacks.

It's much easier being a cat, thought Library Cat as he slipped under the glass doors and into the foyer and immediately into the cooing welcome of a beaming librarian.

"Morning, Library Cat! Here's some bacon. D'aw, aren't you cute!"

Indeed, thought Library Cat, his fur bristling at the condescension. *Kindly don't judge me on my looks alone.*

Curving his back under the Human's stroke, Library Cat quickly devoured the bacon and slinked away to head for the Towsery.

There are Towseries in libraries all over the world. Many Humans would have it that the only reason cats are attracted to libraries is for comfort. They are, after all, warm with many slow-moving, unthreatening Humans who are happy to offer tickles and provide titbits. In reality, this is only half the reason why thinking cats like Library Cat are irresistibly attracted to libraries. What Humans fail to realise is that, for a thinking cat, a library plays much the same role as it does for a thinking Human: it is a receptacle of knowledge, a bricked container of a thousand thoughts and ideas. Generations of thinking cats, much like Library Cat, have tried to position themselves among the ranks of the Human readers, and have headed directly for the stacks of books and boxes of books, only to be shooed away by spectacle-wearing, broom-brandishing, lilac-donning librarians.

Just because we don't speak doesn't mean we're incapable of thought, Library Cat had mused on such occasions, his eyes glowering.

As a result, at some point during the last century, and around the time of T. S. Eliot's seminal work on cats, there had been a kind of feline uprising. Thinking cats began to revolt. Unbeknownst to Humans, they began to pioneer their own, unlimited, underground access to literature. Their method? Well, that's magical and a closely guarded secret. But rest assured that in every library frequented by a cat across the globe, there is a secret stack of books hidden out of sight, known only as 'the Towsery'.

The Towsery is warm. It is often located high up in the eves of a library, where cobwebs, wooden beams and joists criss-cross above the cats' heads. It is bright, with stunning views. Often, there are windows that are small and low to the ground, so that the thinking cat may gaze out, if he wishes, in order that he may more thoroughly ruminate upon the particular book he is currently engrossed in. Library Cat loved these windows. The Towsery in the Edinburgh University Library had wonderful views: in winter, there are the snow-covered Pentland Hills, breaking thickly like waves across the horizon. In May and June, there are the Meadows directly beneath and the Humans having barbecues, the very smoke from which seeming to christen the onset of summer's lease. In spring there's pink blossom in the gutters, and quick-paced Humans heading to the library to revise, while right now – autumn – everything becomes amber as leaves start to fall unveiling the criss-cross of paths in the Meadows and the Humans upon them scurrying to and fro like tiny little mice. And at a cat's eye line, at all times of the year, were the chimneypots, extended out in all directions like blond fields of newly sliced wheat. A good Towsery has a decent supply of bugs and birdlife, and the Towsery at Edinburgh University Library boasted a plentiful supply of these things, and was particularly famed for its pigeon and spider. A good Towsery would have a good alpha – a Towser, as he or she is known – to ensure plentiful supplies of catnip, regular supervision against overwork and protection against Human interference.

It may not come as a surprise, Human, that Library Cat was the incumbent Towser at Edinburgh University Library.

"But where do the books come from?" you may ask.

Well, to answer that question, we must turn to the librarians!

For centuries, librarians have been plagued by mysteries: disappearing books, curiously accrued fines, unlabelled books, books with pages missing, books positioned in odd places, books with things written in the margins… On many such occasions, students have been wrongly blamed, and had their accounts locked and their graduations postponed until the book has been returned, replaced, cleaned, repositioned or reordered. How little both parties know! How much false blame has been issued! How little they know that pernicious thinking cats have been at work, prodding books off the return trolleys and dragging them under the stacks, and that the curiously "mislaid" item has instead ended up in the dustiest, furriest, most hidden corner of the library's Towsery, perused by clandestine groups of incognito thinking cats.

Serves the Humans right for their carelessness, thought Library Cat this morning, as he slinked quietly behind the helpdesk and headed for the Towsery.

Half an hour later, he emerged back into the foyer, having primed his mind for a good few hours of Human-watching. This morning, the first thing he noticed was the speed with which they were all moving. Darting in all directions across the foyer were frantic, fresh-faced students, earnestly heading up stairs and clutching books, some of them tripping, some of them speaking quickly in lilting voices with an especial fondness for the word "like". Library Cat eavesdropped on one particular conversion:

"Yeah, like, I was like sooo hung-over after Hive last night? Like, I was in my lecture and like so wanted to chunder, but like couldn't…?"

Are they speaking another language? thought Library Cat, confused. *And why are they ending every sentence with a strange inflection, as if everything's a question? And what's this about a "Hive"?*

Irritated, Library Cat slinked through the crowd, many of whom didn't even notice him, and trod terrifyingly close to his tail. Then, disaster struck. As he turned the corner towards his turquoise chair in the foyer, he found it occupied by a student Human, who cavalierly sat in it while chewing gum, utterly ignorant to the fact that it was his, was covered in his hair, and was reserved indefinitely for his furry posterior alone. Library Cat became enraged. Wide-eyed and pursed-up, he ventured out into the fresh cold autumn air. And then it hit him.

They've arrived, he thought. *The Freshers are here; that's one sitting on my turquoise chair.*

Over the years, Library Cat had grown quite accustomed to recognising a Fresher. Since his reading habits eschewed all knowledge of the university's academic timetable, Library Cat was forced to find other means of recognising Freshers. This wasn't too difficult, as the typical Edinburgh University Fresher usually betrayed themselves relatively quickly through certain mispronunciations that could not go unnoticed by a fastidious, all-listening-and-thinking cat such as himself. Examples of these mispronunciations included:

1. Pronouncing Teviot as "Tevv-i-yot".
2. Pronouncing Buccleuch Street as "Buck-Looch Street".
3. Pronouncing Ceilidh as "Ker-lye-der".
4. Pronouncing Potterrow as "Potter-rowe".

Other giveaways were:

5. Wandering into the library and asking "Is this 'The Advice Place'?"
6. Tedious displays of machismo.
7. References to Harry Potter while gazing up wide-eyed at buildings.
8. Laughter at the fact some buses terminate at a place called "Bush".

(*I really don't see what's drôle about the word "Bush"*, thought Library Cat. *A bush is a perfectly charming creation.*)

Suddenly, there was a voice:

"Oh my God, is that Library Cat!?"

"What?"

"There's apparently this thinking cat who lives here called Library Cat!"

"Are you on MDMA?"

"No seriously!"

Library Cat eyed the Humans suspiciously. He felt uncomfortable, and overcrowded, his personal space compromised. He wandered into the long grass of George Square to muse on what he'd seen.

They appear to not understand how a library operates, he thought. *Whatever happened to pondering… to learning gently as learning should be undertaken? If only they could see the Towsery. They seem to be subjecting themselves to never-ending psychological torment.*

Library Cat knew that the Human libraries used to be much like the Towsery. But then something called 'Education Reforms' happened. Universities started to be sausage factories for the middle-class literati – feeder schools for Penguin Books and PricewaterhouseCoopers. And also, they were no longer free: Library Cat could wander into the Towsery whenever he wished, but apparently these student Humans had to pay great sums of money for the privilege of even crossing the library's threshold! As such, the Humans often had to work several jobs in order to pay for access to university and the library.

They're doing too much! thought Library Cat. *They'll burn out! And they need to stop using the word "like" unnecessarily.*

Then Library Cat had an epiphany: *Maybe if they stopped repeating the word "like" unnecessarily, they'll free up a lot of time. With this time, they can then learn to study properly and take it from there.*

And so Library Cat, self-satisfied in the belief that he'd got his quest to better understanding the Human off to a good start, headed back home to the chaplaincy.

Enough for one day, he thought as he kneaded his paws in and out of his bed, lapped up some milk, had a scratch of the skirting board and gently fell off to sleep.

❧ Recommended Reading

Life's Little Instruction Book by H. Jackson Brown.

❧ Food consumed

1 x piece of bacon; 1 x woodlouse (in the Towsery).

❧ Mood

Very Good, though chequered with irritation.

❧ Discovery about Humans

They've forgotten how to be calm, and forgotten how libraries work.

Roadworks

...in which our hero
watches pointless digging

The next morning, Library Cat awoke with a start. From out in the square, there came a horrendous noise. It made his ears twist back. The Humans were up to something. A peculiar odour seeped in through the gap under the window that smelt like burning and rubber mixed together.

It sounds and smells like the fourth circle of Hell, winced Library Cat, *this is what Dante had in mind, I'm sure.*

He rose and arched his back, blearily stretching his paws before him and lumbered blearily out on to the street to investigate. There in front of him were a variety of Humans, many dressed in bright yellow, while wrestling with pieces of wire and pipe next to a big hole in the ground. They seemed to have dug up a portion of the road for no apparent reason whatsoever. To his right, there was a massive red van from which a great heat seemed to radiate sideward. It was so intense that it almost singed Library Cat's fur. Inside it, he could see a furnace releasing silky plumes of smoke that unfurled into the sky. Beneath the furnace, there poured a thick back gloop that thudded into a vat like treacle.

A memory stirred. *I remember them from before! They were digging up the same bit of road last week. Why are they back?*

But what was most curious was the sign. Adjacent to all the commotion, the Humans had erected a big triangular notice. To most cats, and Humans, this sign would say "Warning: Human at Work". To Library Cat, the sign said, "Warning: Incompetent Human Struggling to Adjust Parasol".

Ridiculous Humans! thought Library Cat. They dig up the road pointlessly, and erect a sign warning each other against their own insipid attempts at garden warfare.

Library Cat rubbed the sleep lazily from his eyes with his paw. Yawning, he walked along the pavement to investigate more. From the other corner of the square, a Human was removing poles that had been attached to the side of tenements and was chucking them into the back of a lorry. With each almighty clang, Library Cat upped his pace into a little canter, looking behind himself in fear.

He couldn't deal with such foolishness, not today, and the annoyance he felt at being woken up as early as 11.14 am still hadn't worn off. He looked at his paws. They were lathered with a thick, black, strong-smelling substance. He licked them and gagged.

He jumped once again as yet another pole was chucked into the back of the lorry.

Why can't they just lay the poles down?

Back by the hole, the yellow Humans were feeding a long, blue pipe underground into which they threaded a long line of cable. The other end of the cable bounced and tweaked with the motion. It made him want to pounce. He edged over to it, claws poised.

But along came another almighty band as more poles were thrown into the back of the van.

This is too much, thought Library Cat. *I can't learn from the Humans if they insist on being insane.*

And with that, Library Cat wrote the day off and slept for another fourteen hours.

❤ Recommended Reading

'Digging' by Seamus Heaney.

❤ Food consumed

Nothing.

❤ Mood

Alarmed.

❤ Discovery about Humans

At times, they show little consideration toward others, with next to no foresight.

Politics

*...in which our hero gets tough
on crime and eats an ant*

A few days later, Library Cat awoke from under a bush in George Square with quite a start. How he ended up in this spot was rather unclear to him.

As he started to think back over the time that had elapsed since the road incident, he suddenly felt a gentle tickle upon his leg.

Strange, he thought. *A tic?* There, indeed, on the side of his white leg was a tiny black tic, quite at home in its new fluffy surroundings. But something else was amiss. Another tickle was coming from under his left paw…

Hesitantly, Library Cat raised the paw to lick the underside but instead was given such a shock that he sprung three foot in the air from his supine position only to land, a split second later, back on all four paws his lemon-yellow eyes widened and his fur thickly fluffed and standing on edge.

Directly beneath where his paw had been, was a tiny hole in the soil, much smaller than that which the Humans were digging the other day. From out of the hole there issued a tiny, thin line of jet-black ants, all marching in single file, advancing in a carefully curved line.

Library Cat was utterly confounded. He didn't know what to do. On the one hand, the line of ants looked like a tiny lace, being tweaked tantalisingly for his delectation, and this made him want to pounce. But on the other hand, at the same time, he knew it wasn't a lace but was in fact a miniature, super-organised army going about some deeply mysterious business, and this made him wary. He edged closer…

Why can't I hear them? Now the ants were disappearing into the thick bracken, unperturbed by its lumpy denseness, like a river insisting upon its natural course through a great, teeming city.

Library Cat sniffed them again. They tickled his nose. This time he sprung even higher. *How do they know they all want the same thing?*

He reversed on his paws, his rear end arching up sharply, not breaking his gaze from the line, feeling quite beaten. This was overwhelming. He hated how nature could be so over-stimulating sometimes! It was so discourteous of it. Nature was there to be eaten or enjoyed, not to bamboozle and sicken like fungus or mysterious ant armies. Time for food; food would help. And milk. And catnip. Yes, catnip would calm him down...

With another inspection of his paw to check it was ant-free, he turned and trotted restlessly out into the street. The pot-hole puddles were beige and muddy with autumn rain, and things smelt damp. But his mood wasn't improving. Something else inexplicable was happening in Edinburgh this morning, this time at the hands of the Humans. Strewn everywhere, like little white sails, were various bits of blue paper with the word 'YES!' written on them. These were joined, in equal amount, with bits of red paper bearing the words, 'NO THANKS!' Some were soggy in the muddy puddles, others were glued to lampposts with other smaller versions of themselves encircling them like a picture frame; many more were in windows, going up and down the tenements; some were on the side of cars; some were even pinned onto the jackets of Humans as little badges...

It seems that the Humans have adopted a new method of talking to each other, mused Library Cat, rather baffled.

Library Cat suddenly thought of the ants, and how coordinated they were, and yet they didn't seem to be talking at all. Instead there was some magical tie between them. It was clear they all wanted the same thing, and they didn't need to keep reaffirming it. They just got on with the job.

I wonder if there are ever any dissenting ants? pondered Library Cat. *Ants that just break from the line because they're not fussed about nectaring up the greedy Queen Ant? Maverick Ants…?*

As he walked along the pavement, his paws ruffling up soggy poster after soggy, and he began to think about how many similar ants in the Amazon might have had their precious homes destroyed and pulped to smithereens to indulge this latest Human fad of mass poster-printing.

Perhaps those ants in George Square were seeking revenge? For all their dispossessed families in the Amazon?

Then it clicked. Big Things must be happening. Biblio Chat had told him all about how *étrange et bizarre* the Humans in his country get when Big Things are afoot, especially a few hundred years ago during a bloody class war called "The French Revolution".

Yes, Big Things. Big Things were definitely happening. Even the ants seemed aware of the Big Things. This no doubt explained why the Edinburgh Humans had stopped talking to each other with their voices and adopted a new, highly equivocal signage-based system (Humans often favoured passive-aggressive modes of communication when it comes to Big Things, it seemed.)

Finally, Library Cat saw a clue that might reveal what all the fuss was about, and the very 'Thing' which was evidently so 'Big'. It was a questionnaire, caught up in one of the sharp fangs of the square's iron railings. He perused it cocking his head to one side:

DO YOU AGREE WITH THE CLOSURE OF THE LIBRARIES?

NO? THEN FOLLOW THE MOVEMENT!

SIGN OUR PETITION!

Forename:

Surname:

Address:

Do You Own Your Property?

Date of Birth:

Ethnic Background:

Orientation:

Closing the libraries! thought Library Cat with alarm, his interest suddenly piqued. *Never. This cannot happen. This MUST NOT happen!*

Suddenly, to his surprise, Library Cat found himself

feeling lighter and more colourful; a Fresher had just stroked him in the correct spot behind the ear, and his ennui had risen and dissipated like smoke in a breeze. He felt energised and impassioned. Yet, as is often the case, he didn't stop to think about how curious it was that a mood can shift so suddenly, and how the slightest fragment of provocative thought was sufficient to achieve this.

I am going to join the movement! he asserted to himself, followed by a loud and sonorous "Meow!" (which, to a Human, translated as "Hark!") He bit the questionnaire off its railing skewer, walked over to the library steps, placed it on the ground and manoeuvred himself square in front of it. With a stretch of his paws, a shake of his haunches, and a twist of his whiskers, he poised himself ready to fill it out.

But then he realised he had a problem. Yes, you've guessed it, Human. He looked down bemusedly at his paws… he didn't have a pen.

I'll "think" the form complete, thought Library Cat, and proceeded to think the form complete as follows.

DO YOU AGREE WITH THE CLOSURE OF THE LIBRARIES?

Having thoroughly considered the adverse effects that library closures would exact upon the serendipitous consumption of discarded bacon rind, I wholeheartedly condemn this move. It would be deleterious. The books? The strokes? The chairs… I mean ARE YOU DAMN MAD?

Forename: *Library*

Surname: *Cat*

Occupation: *Cat*

Address: *Library*

Date of Birth: *The early twenty-first century*

Do You Own Your Property? *If I sit on it, then yes.*

Ethic Background: *Black & White / Thinking Cat*

Orientation: *Currently west-facing.*

Library Cat felt satisfied. Getting his feelings out made him feel much better. His breathing that had formerly been elevated with excitement began to settle down again. He looked around at the other Humans to see how they were reacting to the news that the library might close. Outside on the library's great concrete forecourt, there was a lot of shouting. Placards were being waved, and people stood at desks with pens and posters trying to accost passers-by. Some appeared to be offering cake to incentivise enrolment.

Others shouted down a megaphone that amplified their voices to the level of a landing jet plane, so that they might outdo those around them who were just talking normally. And in the middle of the fracas, a man with a grey beard walked up and down with a board over his front and back shouting that all these ideas were phony and that everyone would go to hell if they didn't stop and talk to him about God instead; but then even he slid behind a desk and tried to tempt people away from the fire and brimstone with a nice cup of warm tea, for which he required a £1 donation.

Library Cat's ears flattened at the jabber of the senseless din. *Why don't they listen to each other, instead of trying to convince others about their own thoughts? Surely they'd learn that their ideas cancel each other out, in the same way that mixing acid with alkali makes water*, mused Library Cat with a certain pompous confidence at his glistening comparison.

He began to feel a little uneasy again. Everyone seemed trapped in their own little bubbles of self-righteousness, while phrases like "common good" and "the people" and "Faslane" flew through the air like tiny javelins. If there was one colour to describe all the people in the scene, it'd be red. And red made Library Cat nervous. Red wasn't his world; his world was the colours of blue and green... possibly with a hint of taupe.

There must be a name given to all this caterwauling, mused Library Cat. *I wonder what it is?*

"Time for a New Politics!" a voice shouted triumphantly.

Library Cat sighed. *It's that "Politics" thing. The time has come again. I guess I should get to the bottom of this politics business once and for all.*

So Library Cat sat down in a muddy urn of daisies next to the library café and adopted the stature of a sphinx, proudly guarding the pyramids and ancient secrets on the banks of the Nile. It was the correct posture for thinking deep things, and Library Cat often adopted the sphinx pose whenever there was an especially challenging concept that needed pondering. It was a kind of mark of respect to the great cats of ancient Egypt.

The great cats who were worshipped as gods by their Human servants as is correct, Library Cat often thought. He closed his eyes, tucked his paws back on themselves, swept his tale close in to his side, and stared to think.

Who was a Politics? And what does a Politics do? he pondered.

It occurred to him over time that a Politics made things called Laws. And Laws stopped the Humans from doing Bad Things. Like Cycling on the Pavement, and selling day-old tuna.

But who actually was a Politics? Let me break the word down… First, there was "Poli-". Well, "Poli-" or "Poly" comes from the Greek prefix "polýs" which means "many", thought Library Cat with satisfaction. *Yes, like "Polycarbonates" means Many Car Bonnets, and "Polyamorous" means many… well… Cat Best Friends… But what about "-tics"?*

Was that not a tic I noticed this morning, on my white paw? Those annoying blood-sucking creatures? Yes, thought Library Cat, looking back it the tiny lump on his white leg, small and firm like a chocolate raison. *I have a tic right here. They have that annoying trait of continually sucking your blood even when you think you've licked them off. And then they grow fatter and fatter on your blood. And then there reaches a point when they're SO engorged by your hard-earned blood – good, honest blood that you've worked hard to nourish and oxygenate – that they eventually drop to the floor dead, martyrs to their own greed...*

Now let's put the words together, thought Library Cat. *"Poli-" and "-tics". "Many Blood Sucking Creatures". The Humans recruit many of these Blood Sucking Creatures to Stop them doing Bad Things. Okay...*

All of a sudden, there was a stir around Library Cat.

"Library Cat, Smile! Wow, this could be your campaign poster!!!!"

"Quick, Get the Library sign in behind him!"

Click

"And again!"

Click

"Smile!"

Click

"Any thoughts on the laws you'd pass, Library Cat?"

Bloodsuckers, thought Library Cat, turning away and heading back to the chaplaincy quite exasperated.

❧ Recommended Reading

Nineteen Eighty-Four by George Orwell.

❧ Food consumed

1 x ant (mistakenly).

❧ Mood

Apathetic. Cynical and lofty.

❧ Discovery about Humans

They tend to value their own beliefs above those of others.

They have "Laws" where cats have intuition.

Puddle Cat

…in which our hero witnesses perfection

In the days that followed the political demonstrations in George Square, heavy rains set in. Library Cat remained indoors. Cars sloshed over the cobbles sending streaks of water down against the panes of his bedroom window. From upstairs, a radio garbled through the day in a sort of post-apocalyptic refrain: "Dogger, severe easterly six to seven, cyclonic in places, good; Forties, Cromarty, Fair Isle, eight to nine, warning of gales later, moderate or good, occasionally poor."

Library Cat was baffled by these strange broadcasts. They seemed to come from another world. Eventually, he ascertained that the broadcasts related to the waters surrounding the United Kingdom and were called "The Shipping Forecast", but he was unsure why they were relevant or to what ends the Humans were to appropriate the information.

Maybe it has rained so much out there that the Humans are being forced to sail to and from their appointments? "Dogger", indeed! It sounds like a horrendous place and I hope never to go there.

However, there was something comforting about the Shipping Forecast. It was like a big warm blanket. As the soft voice wafted downstairs and the rain beat ever harder on the windows and gurgled ceaselessly down the gutters, Library Cat imagined he was a ship's cat aboard a great galleon, bound for lands afar where he would uncover great culinary and literary treasures. Part of him hoped the rains would never stop, and that in sleep, he'd merge with his dream. But stop they did. A few days later, the rains waned, and Library Cat ventured outside to stretch his legs, refreshed from proper sleeps, and feeling really quite good in himself. Along the gutter, silvery puddles reflected the white sky above with crystal clarity.

A sudden thirst struck Library Cat, and he sauntered off the kerb towards one of the puddles for a drink. All of a sudden, as he looked into the puddle, he became utterly spellbound.

Library Cat had never given much thought to the subject of love. Last Valentine's Day he'd concluded, after some thought, that "The Valentine"… was a purely Human concept perfectly befitting that specie for whom copulation only occurred on 14th February each year, and who saw fit, on this day, to buy each other odd pre-copulation gifts such as candles that released poisonous fumes, and terrifyingly turgid red bags of air that floated around hallways making unearthly bangs when touched by a clawed paw.

And then it hit him. Love. It shot into focus like a humungous telescope, bringing into his vision the eternal, infinite colours of the universe. The stars in all their yellow brilliance. The soft blue swirls of Neptune. The deep, red, towering supernovas. And who was the cat that had caused such tectonic stirring? Who was the cat that had finally kindled love in our hero's tiny, feline breast? PUDDLE CAT!

Puddle Cat was beautiful, with a shiny coat and long whiskers. Puddle Cat was stunning. Library Cat was in love. Suddenly the world around Library Cat seemed to dissolve; all but himself, Puddle Cat and a sprouting autumnal narcissus remained. He'd forgotten all about his drink of water.

He walked back the chaplaincy holding the image like a red laser dot, flickering and ungraspable. His heart beat hard. He felt delicious as the thought of Puddle Cat washed over him.

He pushed his way through the cat flap and into his bed, and there he stayed, kept awake by his own purring.

❧ Recommended Reading

'Sonnet 18' by William Shakespeare.

❧ Food consumed

Dissolved piece of mud.

❧ Mood

Enraptured.

❧ Discovery about Humans

They trivialise perfection.

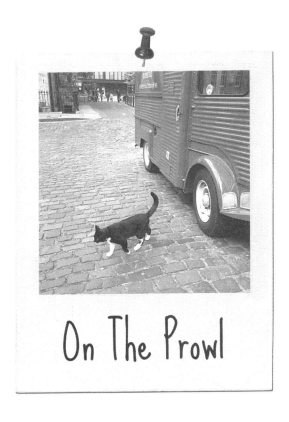

On The Prowl

*...in which our hero heads out
for a night down the alleys*

A week later, Library Cat awoke to the colour of orange. It was 1st October and autumn had well and truly descended. Browns and ambers mixed deeply together among the littered leaves, and the very whirrs and hums of the city seemed to braid beautifully into their papery shuffle along the pavement.

A cornucopia of delicateness, thought Library Cat, his two front paws on the edge of the windowsill with just his ears and eyes poking above into the square. *How pleasing!*

Things had gone quiet and Library Cat could only assume that the Humans had finally agreed on which set of "bloodsucking creatures" should make the new "laws" which governed the fate of day-old tuna.

Thank goodness for that, mused Library Cat, relieved that his choice to keep his views to himself could no longer be denunciated as apathetical. Still uppermost in his mind, however, was the beautiful image of Puddle Cat – the first she-cat to instantly win over his heart.

Oh Puddle Cat! Was the image of a cat ever more lovely and temperate? thought Library Cat, freely quoting Shakespeare because he's out of copyright. *Oh Puddle Cat! You were like my best side! The missing piece to my puzzle… Am I really to see you just the once? You mimicking my every move in reverence? Your coat rippling in the breeze?*

Library Cat was so carried away in his own soppy cloud of love that he almost failed to hear the rustle in the hallway: a postcard had fallen just inside the cat flap. Jumping down, he weaved his way past his piles of books and out into the long, cold corridor, its floor glowing with little parallelograms of autumn sunlight.

He looked at the postcard on the mat. It was from his English cousin, Saaf Landan Tom:

Cuz –

Been finking about ya, mate. Hope ya well and that. Howz about I hit up your gaff in Edinbrah, and we go mousing one day? Also, I need to take you On The Prowl... Serioussssslee, mate, I can't believe you've never been On The Prowl. The nights in Edinbrah are wicked, mate, just wicked. I'll take you when I'm up – da alley scene up near you is bangin' mate, I'm tellin' ya'. Tons of byoo'tiful she-cats. We can cotch at yours, go to the Towsery, read sum naughty books, do some nip and head out on the town, yoo wiv me, yeah? YEAH!

Also I need to cotch wiv you coz I totally forgotten where I live. And this sofa I'm sleeping on under this bridge is bare itchy, mate. And the rats here are MASSIVE.

Cheers, cuz, you da cat.

Yours presumptuously,

Saaf Landan Tom

Saaf Landan Tom was only half thinking cat. From his father's side (whoever his father was), Saaf Landan Tom came from pure alley cat stock, whose lineage dated back to the Great Plague. For a pedigree thinking cat like Library Cat, his cousin's uncouth behaviour could at times be a little bit hard to endure. Saaf Landan Tom had no style. No panache. No *esprit de chat* as Biblio Chat would say.

But Library Cat's cockney cousin had his advantages. Catnip was always in plentiful supply when his cousin was present, and whenever Library Cat was thinking a little too much – his mind white hot and overloaded with knowledge – Saaf Landan Tom was the perfect cat to bring him back to earth.

Also Saaf Landan Tom never arrived empty pawed. Whether it was rat, vole, mouse or a how-on-earth-did-you-kill-that badger, Saaf Landan Tom always announced his visit with the most succulent and freshest killing one could imagine. It was hard for Library Cat not to soften against his cousin's grating habits and unrelenting insistence for "fun" when he arrived with such delicious offerings, such potent catnip and such saucy suggestions for literature.

Hmmmmm, thought Library Cat, reading over his cousin's postcard once again. *As long as he doesn't stay for weeks and besmirch my rug with fur balls, I will accept him. But going out On The Prowl? Never. I'm just not that kind of cat...*

Library Cat thought back to the one and only other time he had gone On The Prowl. It had been an unmitigated disaster. He had been sitting in his turquoise chair one day, and a Human had approached and said, "Looking hot, Library Cat! Would you be my Valentine?"

From this comment, Library Cat had gleaned that the Human was trying to tell him it was time for love, and that he should drag himself out On The Prowl. And so he did. He'd eaten well, and licked his coat until it shined. He'd caught the finest rodents, as offerings. *They should be so lucky*, he'd thought, looking down at the clutch of maimed mice he'd amassed. Then, he'd retched up a fur ball (no cat wants to be gagging on a fur ball when he's about to seal the deal with a beautiful she-cat), took a brief drink of water, gnawed his collar off and headed out the cat flap at 4 am, ready to join the hoard of other cats mewing their way down the alleys towards night-time pleasures.

But when he arrived at the spot, beneath a flickering sodium streetlight, Library Cat just couldn't do it. He tried to get involved, but was invariably shunted to the side to watch other cats nuzzle each other's noses and nip each other's ears affectionately, which made his tail fat with jealousy. (This was because Library Cat knew all this nuzzling, and coat-preening, and mouse-giving was all a big preamble to… well… you-know-what. And frankly, Library Cat was terrible at you-know-what.) Library Cat had tried to ruin the mood by hissing from his sideline position, but it hadn't worked. Chemistry is chemistry after all. Eventually he quietly gathered his mice-offerings up by their tails, walked over to another cat's house and dumped them on his doorstep, before tiptoeing quietly out into the street pondering banal things like, *I wonder why "alleys" are called "closes" in Scotland?* and *What on earth is a "Fire Hydrant"?* and *Why aren't they bothered by the threat of stray dogs, and traffic, and catching worms, and lice and, and, and…*

No, I'm not going to let that happen again, resolved Library Cat, his ears twitching backwards at the recalled embarrassment of it all, and the added humiliation he'd feel once more if it were to happen again in front of his alley cat cousin and highly seasoned prowler.

He took the postcard in his mouth and sat back down for a little snooze to await Tom's arrival, but no sooner had he stopped kneading his cushion, pleasantly allowing the image of Puddle Cat to wash over him, than there came through the gap under the window, the unmistakable tuneless screech of alley cat, followed promptly by the cat flap going.

Well, that'll be him then, thought Library Cat, arching his back with a disgruntled flash in his eyes, and sure enough around the corner swaggered his South London cousin.

Saaf Landan Tom was twenty full pounds of pure, swaggering cockney wide-cat – coarse ginger fur, a few nips bitten out his left ear from various fights he'd endured and a black spot on his tail where a Parcel Force lorry had started its engine while he was gnawing on a kebab skewer beneath its tailgate. And here he was now, on this chilly, yellow Edinburgh autumn morning, marching into Library Cat's home, givin' it all that.

"Meow," said Library Cat frostily.

"Eow!" replied Saaf Landan Tom with cheer.

"Meow," responded Library Cat, determined not to succumb to his cousin's sloppy diction.

"EOO!!" replied Saaf Landan Tom, loud and unperturbed.

This was not a good start. The interaction triggered more memories in Library Cat's mind about his cousin's dastardly habits.

The first issue – Saaf Landan Tom had fleas. Many fleas. It was a blight he'd picked up from his tendency to rest his furry posterior on any discarded, offensively maroon three-piece suite he could find – a pastime which regularly saw him skulking the perimeters of civil amenity centres as far north as Elephant & Castle. But worse, Saaf Landan Tom sprayed. Everywhere. On Library Cat's food, his scratch post, his bed, his rug, his secret stash of catnip… Library Cat had even taken to burying his precious *Complete Works of Friedrich Nietzsche* in his own litter tray since it might be the only place where Saaf Landan Tom didn't spray. No avail. Saaf Landan Tom sprayed there too. Saaf Landan Tom had apologised in good nature; claimed it was all down to habit, innit… but then continued anyway.

What tumultuous hells am I to undergo this time? fretted Library Cat, nonchalantly nudging his food bowl in the direction of his cousin in a strained act of generosity while watching on, with straight-backed composure, as his enormous cousin voraciously wolfed down the chunks of food between sonorous, deeply satisfied purrs, only to follow up the meal by lapping from the adjacent water bowl contaminating it with greasy lumps of jellied chicken. As the great cat finally finished, he nudged the bowl in Library Cat's direction and his cousin took a few delicate nibbles, half in awe and half resentful of the massive virile hulk of ginger tomcat beside him.

As the evening wore on, Library Cat's anger softened. The two cats had passed a pleasant early evening in the Towsery, and the catnip, milk, mice and literature had flowed pleasingly. Library Cat saw Tom in a different light – a deeply intelligent cat with a visceral, red-blooded exterior, and Library Cat was rather admiring of the urbane way in which his cousin could flit between one character type and the other, and yet never seem disingenuous or fake in doing so. He was truly the best of both worlds: thinker by day, prowler by night.

It was early evening by the time both cats headed out of the Towsery having indulged a broad selection of literary tastes, and set off through the foyer of Edinburgh University's Main Library, and down the concrete steps to a desolate George Square. Saaf Landan Tom led the way, his great tail towering above his cousin's nose like a massive ginger toilet brush that had become rather unpleasantly matted.

I'll go out for half an hour, thought Library Cat, *but no more. I have a lot of reading to do tomorrow...*

Further and further they walked, down the plumbing of streets, wynds and closes. Library Cat began to feel cold. Evening advanced suddenly, like a pack of black playing cards being dealt across a table. Library Cat could feel the ominousness of night enveloping the very nation, top to bottom, closing in on faraway fields and shores, and now creeping up on them in Edinburgh – on Bristo Place and Candlemaker Row – cloaking up the lights, allowing only the little yellow halos of certain street lamps to burn determinedly through the fog in shimmering rings… they towered above Library Cat like beacons on top of skyscrapers. Colours became ashen. Suddenly, in the corner of his eye, he caught glimpses of cats skulking. They were evidently out On The Prowl too. One could just tell by the way they moved, somehow. Library Cat's nerves heightened. Things felt crepuscular. Suddenly he found himself thinking of Robert Louis Stevenson and *Jekyll and Hyde*, and wondered whether cats could have evil counterparts that stalk the night-time streets as well.

I'm going back, he thought. *I don't want this. I want to think about Puddle Cat in my cosy warm room. Tom's clearly trying to take me properly out On The Prowl. I shall resist. I am really just not that type of cat.*

Discreetly, Library Cat slowed his pace, and was about to turn around and break into a gallop. But no sooner did he falter than his cousin purred and mewed loudly, luring Library Cat on with the false promise of nearby mice. Library Cat knew he was most likely bluffing, but then the possibility of a nearby rodent is a temptation that Catkind finds virtually impossible to ignore. After all, the deliciousness of food trumps the wonder of thought, even for a purebred thinking cat like Library Cat.

Soon the pair turned the corner into an alley. It had the soft bite of intrigue that all cut-through alleys in Edinburgh have. A sign bearing the name "Heriot Place" glimmered whitely on an ancient black and brown wall that itself was labelled "Telfer Wall" in ornate, gold letters. The air was lambent with catnip and scent marking. Ahead of them, the alley stretched out threateningly, its wet, narrow pavement gleaming like steel in the reflection of the full moon above. About halfway down, Library Cat could see a group of cats huddled beneath a flickering light. As they advanced closer, Library Cat glanced up at the enormous tenement buildings either side and wondered in which direction he'd bolt if things turned sinister. It was either back down to the main road the way he'd arrived, or straight ahead into the deeper, darker gloom of the unknown. Dogs barked in the distance; a few Humans nearby smashed something glass on the floor.

Finally, the pair arrived.

Library Cat eyed the cats in the group. It was immediately evident which one was attractive to him. In the corner, half-concealed by bracken, a small tortoiseshell sat wide-eyed beneath an electric meter. Her paws were extended down determinedly in front of her as if she was trying to resist being pushed forward from behind. Quickly, Library Cat preened his face and the backs of his paws, and with adrenaline rushing through him, stood up and trotted over to the tortoiseshell. He sat down in front of her. Holding Library Cat's glance, the tortoiseshell purred melodically and began rolling her snake-like coat over and over on the muddy path, a white paw outstretched celestially towards Library Cat like God's hand breathing life into Adam in Michelangelo's *Creation*. Library Cat was transfixed. He didn't know where to look. *This is amazing!* He trotted over and nuzzled her. Her fur felt like silk. For a moment he smelt the sweet stagnancy of her breath. It was tinged with the reek of a Sheba terrine. The purrs of the two cats harmonised for one moment. One blissful time-stopping moment.

But then all became strange. The tortoiseshell flinched, suddenly, and became wide-eyed. A certain awkwardness stole through the air. The two cats surveyed each other silently for a moment. Library Cat didn't know what to do. A weird heat started to rise inside of him from the sheer embarrassment. What had gone wrong? *Do something, do something, Library Cat*. The awkwardness was terrible. This couldn't go on. Finally, with a de-clawed paw, Library Cat gently biffed her on the side of her back while uttering the only icebreaker line he knew: "Prrrrrrrrp?"

Almost instantaneously, the tortoiseshell quadrupled in size. Her fur extended out into the air, and her cavernous mouth opened brutishly to reveal a long track of fangs through which she spoke a deep, spitting, sibilant hiss, swiping her paw against his side, before darting down the close and into the gloom.

Well, that went well, thought Library Cat, as certain other members of the cat fraternity turned to eye him, standing alone, his paw still outstretched. Two amorous white cats looked up from their canoodling. A ginger, eating a mouse, paused mid-chew and gazed over. A clutch of tiny mewing shorthairs, suspiciously young and probably still within kittenhood, played boisterously over the silence. Finally, breaking the stasis, a green-eyed alley began walking towards Library Cat poised-of-claw, but thought better of it as Library Cat rose sharply to his feet and growled him down.

"Grrrrrrrooaaaaaaaaaarrrrrrrrrroooooooooooooooooooow wwwwww…"

And then it happened. Suddenly the scene became a throbbing ball of fur, fangs and noise. Hisses, scratches, swipes and bites all tumbled over each other as Saaf Landan Tom – originally enjoying the company of an amorous she-cat near a litterbin – bounded into the middle of the scene like a lion, thrashing this way and that.

And then nothing. Library Cat was alone. The alley was empty, with the cats seeming to have evaporated into thin air. He had no idea where they had all gone, and was loath to cry for Tom, lest the baying throng stampeded back for some reason. A dog barked nearby. He shivered. Looking down at his paw, he noticed a few red beads of blood beginning to plush up on its white tip like tiny berries. He dunked it down in a nearby puddle to wash it.

And then he saw her again. *PUDDLE CAT!* Her whites ripped and silver; her blacks velvety and ethereal; her eyes flickering like emeralds and her whiskers like white lace;

and her expression seeming to speak the secrets of a thousand interminable years of knowledge and wisdom.

Library Cat was speechless and, more to the point, thought-less. Gently with the sweet-terror of a Petrarchan prince, he moved his mouth closer to the image. (*She moved in too! Oh the joy!*) He wanted to contain the moment forever but couldn't think how. Could he kiss her? He must kiss her. *I have to kiss her!* And with that, he lowered his head down to hers, and was just about to rub his cheek against her soft head when…

"Eow!"

Saaf Landan Tom jocularly sat down in the puddle sending a raft of muddy ripples fleeing in all directions from the sheer bulk of his enormous fluffy backside. He had something in his mouth. It was a note:

Sorry about that mate. Not what I planned. Home?

As the two cats wended their way back along Lauriston Place, their breath pluming little clouds of condensation in front of them, Library Cat began to feel a little… how might we put it… unusual. He had only had a few snickets of catnip, and was initially feeling a little woozy and lightheaded – a perfectly normal response. But now things were turning strange. Objects began to take on the shape and fluidity of a Salvador Dalí painting, with melting colours and sounds.

Fireflies seemed to buzz above his head, and he found himself bounding up joyfully to snap at them only for them to disappear into the black. Traffic lights and dustbins suddenly seemed to gain an alarming and inexplicable sentience. All of a sudden, shimmering in front of his eye line, he could see himself linking with Puddle Cat in an ensouled room, red with light and ablaze with bitter sublimation. Her black fur was interminably deep like jet, while her white fur was glowing moon-silver like platinum. Now she emerged purring through the gloom to Library Cat on the street, nuzzling him gently. And then they were eating mice after it had happened, and then… nothing… All images vanished as a diorama of blackness passed across his vision.

❧ Recommended Reading

Trainspotting by Irvine Welsh.

❧ Food consumed

Watery lumps of jellied chicken, a mouse, half a lamb kebab, and some grade-one catnip.

❧ Mood

Heady excitement, to delirious, to a crushing nihilistic disappointment.

❧ Discovery about Humans

Their abuse of chemicals at night isn't as incomprehensible as previously thought.

Shame

*…in which our hero recalls the night
before, and eats potentially poisonous tuna*

Shame. That's what Library Cat felt right now. Pure, unadulterated cat shame.

He had been sick. On his turquoise chair in the library. The vomit clearly contained the dark brown threads of the previous night's catnip. His memory of the night was a blur.

There had been Puddle Cat, and a beautiful tortoiseshell, he remembered that much, but that was all. Now his lamentable loss of dignity in the sober surroundings of the library led to him being shooed out into the cold square.

My head feels like a lead ball, thought Library Cat, the effects of last night's debauchery forcing him into the heady heights of metaphor.

But there was more. An hour of so earlier, Library Cat had headed home only to discover Saaf Landan Tom drinking from his water bowl once again, contaminating it with large chunks of chicken jelly. And then something terrible happened. Library Cat lashed out. For the first time in his life, the red mist had descended. Incensed by his cousin's boorish impertinence, and still fat-tailed with jealousy over Tom's evidently more successful time On The Prowl the night before, Library Cat had dealt his cousin a smart blow to the neck, with all five claws fully deployed. It was over in an instant. Saaf Landan Tom had fled the house and Edinburgh hissing curtly, his great ginger tail swishing through the air like a medieval torch.

This was worse than the vomit in the library. This was worse than ostracism to the square. This was a slight of character. Up until this point, Library Cat had fought all his wars with two deeply coveted weapons – weapons of infinite virtue, that brought their bearers certain victory against cats and Humans alike, and which were brandished by thoroughbred thinking cats all over the world. The two weapons were: thoughts and expressions. They'd never failed Library Cat before and, he assumed, they never would. But he'd swiped, there was no escaping the matter. And it was his own flesh and blood at the receiving end – his dear, well-meaning half-thinking cat cousin, Saaf Landan Tom. For a thinking cat to engage in warfare at all is a slight of character; but for a thinking cat to lash out rather than stare down or outsmart brings even greater embarrassment to the thinking cat community. And yet the only thought Library Cat had had at the time was, to put it succinctly, *Take that you slobbering, ginger, nip-addled, toilet-brush-tailed b*****d!*

Library Cat looked mournfully at the trees in the square and at the tiny fractals of ice that were beginning to encircle their boughs as the teeth of winter sank deeper into the land. Beyond, he could see the Humans in their tenement houses, moving to and fro in their yellow-warm lounges behind world-muting glass. This was definitely the lull after the drama – the cold, cobble-contemplating lull, the bleak, autumnal, dank tumbleweedy solitude. Library Cat almost felt as if the weather was conspiring to make him feel even guiltier.

What came over me? Oh, the humiliation. Vomit and a swipe on the same day!

His long held dream of becoming university rector cat seemed to slither away before his eyes.

Is this the cat I've become? Am I to live a life punctuated with violence and covert catnip deals beneath flickering street lamps? Shunned by thinking cats, and exiled from the delicious warmth and literary pleasures of the Towsery?

"Yo! Cat! Hey, wait up!"

A Human was running towards him, his red satchel bouncing off his waist. Just as Library Cat thought he'd stop, he continued running past him.

Fine, run on by me sir, your indifference means nothing to me, seethed Library Cat inwardly.

But now another Human, a girl this time, approaching him more slowly.

"Hey Library Cat! Hey, come here…"

She bent down and kissed the air in his direction. Pleased for the company, Library Cat rose and moped over, avoiding eye contact.

"There, there, no need to look so sad! Here, have some tuna."

TUNA!

"There, there. Good boy."

BOY? … hmmm strokes, yes, strokes, strokes, strokes… mm… KEEP STROKING!

"More? OK, here you go."

No, not more Tuna, you cretin, more strokes!

"Mmm? No more? OK… Your coat is so soft…!"

YES! Strokes… Mmmm… strokes. That last stroke was scrummy.

The Human eventually rose, towering up above him, turned and walked away smiling. Then the night before came flooding back to Library Cat once more.

But it had disappeared for a moment. During the strokes, his mind had become unstuck. It had lifted away, beyond the past and lingered in the present. For a second, he had forgotten about the last twenty-four hours.

It was a start.

❧ Recommended Reading

'Whatever Happened' by Philip Larkin.

❧ Food consumed

1 x lump of tuna (probably more than a day old so technically "illegal").

❧ Mood

Cyclonic. Slowly stabilising.

❧ Discovery about Humans

Sometimes, they are a much-needed distraction.

Proximate Bird

*...in which our hero
reasons with a raven*

Still extradited from the library some hours later, Library Cat had taken to sleeping on the concrete benches just outside the library café. It was better than nothing. But cold concrete is a poor substitute for the lavish turquoise fabric of his usual chair in the foyer.

His tummy heavy with tuna, he had just dozed off into a tail-twitched sleep when he was rudely awoken.

"Squark," said the Proximate Bird.

Oh shut up, thought Library Cat.

"Squark! Squark!," said the Proximate Bird, with vigour.

Look it's quite simple, seethed Library Cat. *I am here to sleep and think; you are here to irritate and be eaten.*

"SQUARK!" repeated the Proximate Bird, unheedingly.

You really are daft, aren't you? Look, I've had a tough forty-eight hours, so let me substantiate what I just thought: I am here to sleep and think. You are here to irritate and be eaten… potentially by me. I kindly draw your attention to the latter part of your measly commission on this earth – the "be eaten by me" part. I accept it's a thought in the passive voice, but…

"SQUAAAAAAAAARK" interrupted the Proximate Bird.

OK that's it, thought Library Cat, *an early dinner it is.*

Library Cat rose, and yawned. He carefully stretched his white paw, and then his black paw, markedly extending his claws each time. He gave his coat a lick (for hunting should never be undertaken with a dirty coat), and shook his head.

If he will insist on interrupting me right while I'm about to have a dream about Nietzsche, mused Library Cat, *then frankly he deserves to be eaten. Right where is he? Proximate Bird? Where are you Proximate Bird? I want to be friends after all. Come now Proximate Bird, I have a worm for you. Proximate Bird…?*

But no sooner did Library Cat rise than Proximate Bird

had flown off to meet his wife, to create many Proximate Chicks, and generally increase the already infuriating din of birds around George Square.

Peace at last! reflected Library Cat. *No birds, no Humans. Bliss! Come at me, Nietzsche.*

He settled back down for a nap.

"Oh my God, yah, the people sitting opposite me on level 4 just WON'T STOP talking, yah. One of them was even SKYPING! Oh Library Cat! Hi Library Cat! Hi! Library Cat, LIBRARY CAT!"

Oh for goodness sake! fumed Library Cat. *The Humans are worse than the birds and they don't even know it!*

❧ Recommended Reading

To Kill a Mockingbird by Harper Lee.

❧ Food consumed

Almost one bird.

❧ Mood

Grossly irritated.

❧ Discovery about Humans

Sometimes, they are utterly blind to their own hypocrisies.

Essay Completion Week

*...in which our hero confronts
what no cat should ever have to confront*

That afternoon saw Library Cat sitting in a ray of sun. Suddenly an intense feeling of imperiousness washed over him. Riding its balmy wave were his father's words, remembered from a time when he was no more than a bounding Library Kitten.

"Everything the light touches, Library Kitten, is your kingdom."

"But what about that far-off shadowy place?" Library Cat had responded.

"That's the Hugh Robson Essay Bunker: you must never go there, Library Kitten."

Hmm, the Hugh Robson Essay Bunker, thought Library Cat now, some six years on. *What's so unpleasant about it, I wonder. And why should I be denied entrance? More to the point, from what archaic law does my untimely forbiddance derive? Biblio Chat had visited it during his last stay in Edinburgh and had claimed it was an "inspiring" experience.*

Then a new thought occurred to him. *What if my father were enacting a kind of subversion to put me off the scent of something exciting? A scent such as... say... books, or MICE? Mice live in bunkers after all.*

Library Cat recognised his thought development as highly stupid and illogical. His relationship with his father had been strange at times but he never really thought him capable of hoodwinking him away from rodents in the manner that was now occurring to him. But the thought of mice had entered his head. And when the thought of mice enter a thinking cat's head, they scurry around in there until their presence is so ubiquitous that the cat in question must seek out a mouse to appease the craving.

And so it was that Library Cat, filled with the image of large, tasty mice, ventured from his sunny, concrete throne beside the library on that late October day, and headed to the enigmatic Hugh Robson Essay Bunker. Down the stairs he went.

All at once a sight of terror met his eyes. Humans typing. Constantly typing! Typing and shuffling notes in a pallid hot void of whirring machines. But worst of all were the mice! There were mice everywhere, but they were strange robotic mice with long, genetically modified tails and no eyes. Each one seemed stunned into enacting the Humans' dastardly deeds, only emitting an eerie "click" as they were dragged across the desks. To hungry Library Cat, they were a parody of temptation.

Get me out, NOW! thought Library Cat, and with that he turned and galloped back up the stairs, crossed the square and resumed his concrete throne.

But the thought stayed with him – the Humans, their robotic rodents complicit and eyeless. Library Cat wanted to shut out what he'd seen, and all its Camus-esque existential hideousness.

Well, at least I now know, thought Library Cat, calming down. *But I think I need a normal mouse to get over this. Mmm, normal mice… Normal tasty mice…*

Library Cat left his concrete plinth and began to stalk the dirty perimeters of the library, keeping his head low and his breathing soft, hoping for a tasty snack.

There! Just in the corner of the library and George Square Lecture Theatre, he spied what he was looking for: a turgid, naïve field mouse snaffling around for crumbs. Library Cat's eyes widened. He tiptoed stealthily forward... one paw down... then the other... and...

"Library Cat, Library Cat! Are your thoughts academically citable?"

From behind him there bellowed the stricken voice of a nervous student.

Obviously they are, I'm Library Cat, thought Library Cat, turning his head back to face the student – a girl smoking and wearing a pashmina scarf – in anger.

"Ya, OK, but which referencing system should I use to cite your thoughts, Library Cat?"

MLA, thought Library Cat.

"Why?"

Because the letter L reminds me of the curvature of a mouse's tail when fleeing in abject fear from my pernicious paw. It stirs me. Now do you mind? I was trying to hunt...

"Thank you, Library Cat, you've helped me a lot!"

Honestly, thought Library Cat exasperated. He turned back just in time to see the mouse's backside disappear down a tiny hole in the concrete behind the library.

And yet another mouse I'll never see again... fumed Library Cat, his ears twisted back in fury.

❖ Recommended Reading

Zen and the Art of Motorcycle Maintenance by Robert M. Pirsig.

❖ Food consumed

(Almost) one mouse.

❖ Mood

Frustrated and cheated.

❖ Discovery about Humans

They are self-absorbed when stressed and should practise feline-inspired mindfulness.

The Arrival of Biblio Chat

…in which our hero
"welcomes" his French cousin

Library Cat watched in horror.

A few yards off, walking imperiously over the cobbles, was his French cousin Biblio Chat. Unlike last year, when Biblio Chat arrived in Edinburgh having given up France for Lent, this year he was on the hunt for a particular book, entitled

Mice and Mousing: Towards a Camusian Phenomenology of the Hunt.

It was difficult to describe the level of hostility Library Cat harboured towards his French cousin. Biblio Chat's jaunty air, his frilly red collar, his late-night *Refléxions de Sartre* (whatever they were) and his showy rejection of Whiskas wet food all stirred a strange rage in him which he could neither fully understand nor control. He was, in deportment and character, the complete antithesis of Saaf Landan Tom.

Honestly, he should take a look at himself, seethed Library Cat as his cousin trotted, high headed, towards him past the David Hume Tower, ignoring the inevitable attention he garnered among those Human students around him by keeping his eyes semi-closed and his head held high as if he might be bathing in a bright ray of sun, while maintaining his trademark Cheshire Cat smile. He didn't so much walk as *glide* and there was something so ethereally learned about him which made Library Cat jealous. Everything about him was preened and shimmering with self-aware Frenchness.

Needless to say, Biblio Chat was spawned from a long line of thoroughbred thinking cats, apparently dating back to the time of the French Revolution (though Library Cat suspected there might've been a bit of alley cat thrown in along the way – an addition that would annoyingly only add to his Gallic charm). It was around this time that his line began a long, deep-rooted alliance with Scotland profiting greatly from the former's academic advances during the Scottish Enlightenment, and gravitating towards their warm public hostelries and rat-infested fourteen-storey tenements. Moreover, Scotland at that time offered refuge for many French thinking cats. When a bloody class war raged forcing the more succulent rodents to flee from the immutable sound of the slicing guillotine, Scotland and its new civilised society of sedentary Adam Smiths, David Humes, William Robertsons, Henry Playfairs and Adam Fergusons offered a welcome oasis for the French thinking cat. Biblio Chat's great grandfather (x 10^4) had been such a cat, and had stowed away on one of the many claret vessels shuttling between Scotland and France at that time. He had ended up being David Hume's cat, and Biblio Chat's line had never forgotten it.

"Reading and sauntering and lounging and dosing, which I call thinking, is my supreme Happiness", Biblio Chat had often postulated, though Library Cat secretly knew that this was a quote of Hume himself, and thus made his cousin a sleekit, devious plagiarist.

But there was one matter that was to forever divide the cousins above all others, no matter how many small periods of *détente* might thaw their tail-widening hostility towards each other when discussing philosophy and literature, and that was food. Mousing with Biblio Chat was an excruciatingly laborious affair. If there was one thing Library Cat couldn't abide it was Biblio Chat's indulgent talk about the experiential qualities of eating and hunting: mouse tones, mouse textures, mouse succulence… mouse tenderness, *maturité, acidité, slainité* and, most loathed of all, *Le Crunch Facteur. You and your Crunch Factor*, thought Library Cat. *Just EAT the damn mouse!*

And then the garlic. Garlic got everywhere when Biblio Chat came to stay. If the rejection of dry food wasn't bad enough, Library Cat had to endure the despicable smell of garlic that could never be completely expunged and seemed to cling to books and bedding as if they'd been touched by the rank hand of some dark, culinary overlord.

Biblio Chat arrived, with a purr, by his cousin's side.

"Meow," said Library Cat, looking in the other direction.

"Miaou," replied Biblio Chat in his own tongue (Library Cat struggled with French).

"Mééiouow", responded Library Cat, attempting his best French accent in the hope of transcending the language barrier.

"Miaou?", replied Biblio Chat, unheedingly.

Library Cat's anger heightened, his tail thickening. *Damn him, he could at least try to speak English!*

"Miaou", replied Library Cat in faux courtesy.

"Miaou! Miaou!" replied Biblio Chat excitedly (clearly Library Cat must've pronounced it right).

And with that, the pair turned and headed towards the library.

It was a quiet morning, around 9 am. Only the most devoted student Humans were at work, touching their matriculation cards on the electronic gates which slid open, and then slid closed leaving a gap, as per usual, that was the perfect width for cat decapitation. The pair carefully slipped under the gates and slinked across the foyer towards the secret entrance to the Towsery. Thinking cats have to exercise extreme caution at the best of times when entering a Towsery – stealth, surreptitiousness and diversion are key assets governing a swift and uneventful entry. Aware of this, Library Cat swiftly started mewing and looking cute. As if from thin air, a gaggle of Humans arrived and began lavishing him with strokes, kisses, tickles and titbits until the library foyer was utterly abandoned, save for one corner where Humans amassed thickly like a swarm of seagulls around a pilchard carcass on a beach. Meanwhile, Biblio Chat slipped into the Towsery unnoticed. Moments later, Library Cat rose and walked off to the exit prompting the gaggle of Humans to disperse, only to double back into the Towsery himself when no one was watching.

The Towsery was beautiful that morning. A musty warm glow shone down the corridor to greet the cats as they limboed under the dusty joists and do-si-doed around the missing floorboards. Cobwebs criss-crossed their path, and as they entered, a warm orange fire greeted them from the hearth in the corner. The high windows parcelled up pieces of grey sky, blurred out by streaks of light rain which coursed down them, making the room seem all the more cosy. Several cats were among the books, or were at play with ribbon bookmarks or paper. A couple more were sleeping by the fire. One or two eyed the newcomer wearily, but Biblio Chat paid them little heed and set about looking for his book.

As the day wore on, the cats wove themselves deeper into the thick silk of knowledge. A pleasant calm fell across Library Cat. He gazed at his cousin between doses, pawing through the papers. *He's true to himself*, he thought. *He might be annoying but he's 100 per cent honest to himself. What is the role of a thinking cat on this earth if not to wallow in knowledge?*

Suddenly Library Cat felt inspired. He wanted to write, he wanted to explore, and above all he wanted to create. A buzzy feeling shimmered down his entire body. He should write a poem! Something with which to woo Puddle Cat if he was ever to see her again: a note he could write and leave nearby her. The Towsery contained many stacks of books by many thinking animals, though the cat and Human books were most prolific among them. Library Cat began nosing the shelves, his whiskers brushing softly against ancient spines that glimmered in the light of the fire. It wasn't long before a book caught his attention: *The GSCE Guide to Creative Writing: Volume 1.*

Seems perfectly serviceable, he thought, raising his paw and pushing the book-lozenge out of the stack, sending it clattering like a Jenga block in a plume of dust the other side. Trotting round he began reading it between sporadic bouts of furious paw licking and daydreaming. It was not very inspiring, and Library Cat began to feel his mood ebb away into an odd mind-turning lassitude.

The problem was not so much with Library Cat, however, but with poetry itself. You see, despite having come across many poems in his life, Library Cat remained indifferent towards pretty much all of them. The idyllic scenes of Wordsworth stirred him not. The thunderous lines of Milton's *Paradise Lost* barely quivered a whisker… Even Shakespeare's sonnets scarcely managed to muster forth a purr from the depths of his ennui-encircled heart.

I just wish I could do it, he thought wearily. A moment later, out of the corner of his eye, he caught a glimpse of some scrawled writing in the margin of the book. The hand was definitely that of a Human, the letters being untidy and seemingly etched into the paper with the belligerence of an inattentive schoolboy. Library Cat's breath stopped as he read the lines again, and again and again. So beautiful were their image upon the mind's eye that Library Cat began purring involuntarily almost as soon as he read them. There was no denying it, Library Cat was stirred. The line read as follows:

The cat sat on the mat.

Such fantastic words! Such genius in their careful choice of imagery, meter and rhyme! Poetry had never before moved

Library Cat so much. Compared to these lines, Wordsworth seemed to whither into a heap of dull, inconsequent near-nonsense – the sort of stuff that might be used to represent poetry at its most boring. He looked around the Towsery. In the corner, by the fire, was indeed a small mat, and with that Library Cat headed over to the mat and rested his furry posterior upon it. Cat – and the mat on which the cat sat – were one; united in a single, emblazoned vision of art. He felt his hostility towards his cousin ebbing away, and replacing it was the timeless joy of art... of reading... of poetry. He was one cat, on one mat. One action... one Muse. Before the moment went, he quickly penned his poem to Puddle Cat, rolled it into a ball, and stuffed it between the thick, gnarled wooden joists of the Towsery.

❖ Recommended Reading

Poetry for Dummies by John Timpane.

❖ Food consumed

Catnip / spider.

❖ Mood

Euphoric, creative.

❖ Discovery about Humans

They can be at their most creative when procrastinating.

Crepuscular

*...in which our hero ponders language
and fears for Humans*

Night had fallen as the two cats nosed their way surreptitiously out of the Towsery and down the long web of narrow, hidden corridors to the library foyer. They were hungry, having only consumed the odd insect all afternoon, and their lust for snoozing and reading had worn thin, as hunger started to replace it, irritating their tummies and diverting their imaginations. Library Cat craved the saltiness of dried food, while Biblio Chat stated his intention for bird, perhaps pigeon – at any rate something *un peu plus délicate* than rodent.

As they nosed their way into the centre of the foyer, however, a sight of horror met their eyes. Students were everywhere in a blur with motion. Some were dropping big fat highlighter pens and papers which fanned out into great carpets of white on the floor; others were dodging each other to get to large grey machines which whirred and spat out yet more papers. The sheer sight of the motion made Library Cat feel queasy. Indeed, everyone was so preoccupied about the business of submitting essays that they hardly noticed Library Cat and Biblio Cat, weaving their double helix among various ankles and shoes, in their irrevocable progression towards the exit. As the cats neared the front door, Library Cat's curiosity got the better of him and he paused to eavesdrop on a telephone conversation.

"Yah, I'm screwed… I'm, like, so screwed. I'm really, really screwed. I was out until, like, four, and then, like, I forgot I had this second deadline for this other essay and, like, now I've got the deadline in, like, TEN minutes. Now I just need to quickly print it. But if I miss the deadline, like, I'm going to be, like, so screwed for this course that I mightaswelljustlike, drop out of uni."

Library Cat was appalled, on many levels, but most markedly

at the student's unrefined rhetoric. He was so appalled in fact that he had to organise his responses to the overheard conversation into the following list:

1 Use repetition and intensifiers sparingly. It would have been sufficient to have just said "I'm screwed" rather than "I'm so screwed", and then, "I'm really, really screwed".
2 Drop some of that ham sandwich you're eating, it looks tasty.
3 Calm down, you'll give yourself an embolism.
4 Address your preoccupation with the word "like".
5 Avoid histrionics. You will be calmer yourself, and seem more sincere, if you avoid pointless, indulgent affirmations of impending failure. It is unlikely a late essay will mean expulsion from university.
6 Tie your shoelaces, they are making me want to pounce.
7 Respect time. Avoid recruiting time simply to ameliorate the terms of your story. Less is more, in this respect.
8 Stop standing by the door, you're letting the cold into the library.
9 Avoid split infinitives: it's 'to print quickly' not 'to quickly print'.

Before Library Cat could think any more there was a tap on the back by another student, this time a man, with a friendly face. Behind him, the door swung shut, and the door in front, where the girl had been standing, swung shut as well.

All at once one of Library Cat's greatest fears had befallen him: entrapment. With the doors immediately ahead and behind closed, he was trapped in a kind of liminal foyer space that served no purpose. And to make matters worse, now this male student was attempting to initiate conversation with him, except he was going about it in a deeply strange manner. Instead of addressing him as a brainless animal in the condescending manner that most Humans do, this student was instead attempting to "talk" in a series of meows and mews and purrs as if this might somehow dissolve the communicative barrier that has endured between cat and Human since the time of the Egyptians, and suddenly prompt Library Cat into a great mellifluous outpouring of reassurance and wisdom that would appease the Human's guilt at having started her essay so late in the day.

"Caticus Domesticus! You don't have to worry about the atomic properties of caesium and all-nighters do you? Lucky wee b*****d. Here, puss, puss, puss, puss! Look at me! Puss, puss, puss. Meow, meeeeow, meeeeeow. Hey UP HERE. Puss, puss, puss, puss, puss..."

Oh jog on, thought Library Cat, seizing the opportunity offered by a Human walking through the main door to make a dash for the square.

Outside, the bitter evening hit Library Cat like a train. An iciness encircled his whiskers making them ridged like little frosted twigs. He scanned the square for Biblio Chat. It wasn't long before he spied his cousin. A little way off, between the black railings, Biblio Chat was enveloped in a cloud of blue-grey features as a scuffle between him and a pigeon ground ever closer to a conclusion. Presently, much to Library Cat's surprise, the pigeon wriggled free, running a feathery zigzag along the grass, until finally lumbering up into the air like a perilously overweight cargo aircraft. Library Cat sniggered inwardly as he watched the very tip of his cousin's tail switch with annoyance. He walked over…

"Meow?"

"Miaou," replied Biblio Chat despondently.

Library Cat's heart softened. He was at once sadistically pleased that his cousin had been outsmarted by a bird, while at the same time sympathetic towards his frustration and defeat. He'd been there after all. All cats had been there. He nuzzled his cousin's coat in an act of kinship. As the two cats walked silently back across the square, both hungry and with the cold cobbles nipping the undersides of their paws, Library Cat thought back to the students and wondered if they ever found time to relax. He had heard it said that students do nothing but relax, but then again, the sight he had just seen thoroughly disproved such an assertion. *Is it that they don't pace themselves? Or oscillate wildly from one extreme to the other? Do they go back to their flats and breathe clear air, free from the demons of anxiety, loneliness and despair that so often unsheathe their invisible daggers in the hideous echoes of silence? Are their homes warm? Are they greeted by nice flatmates? Or are they met with a blaze of ice, slamming doors and passive-aggressiveness? A closed-room culture of segregated fridge compartments and alienation?*

A sudden sadness hit Library Cat. He had a horrible feeling that the Humans had forgotten how to live. He had been to the neighbouring Edinburgh districts of Marchmont and Sciennes on adventures sometimes. They had seemed, superficially at least, quite wonderful. He'd gazed up at ambient rooms where posters of *Le Chat Noir* hung beneath fairy cake ceiling cornices and thought these student Humans are doing it right. He'd walked along the moss-linted pavement and watched cars quaintly lumber over the street humps, their wheels on the cobbles sounding like waves washing up the seashore. The tenements at night faced each other serenely, some bandaged in scaffolding, others adorned with moulded cornucopia that illuminated ethereally in the moonlight. Everything was tinged with a lovely flavour; it was the flavour of *elsewhere*.

But sometimes, Library Cat would hear the local cats discuss ownership in their electrically synthed voices and suddenly feel uneasy and out of place. It was not his territory after all. The scents were all different, none of them his. *Was that why it could feel so lovely and magical? And did the Humans feel the same way? Or did they only feel the sudden estrangement of the whining cats... the unmistakable feeling that they don't belong?*

Back inside the chaplaincy, Library Cat and Biblio Chat sat down to dinner. Suddenly Puddle Cat came to mind, and Library Cat felt particularly proud that he had gone several hours today without thinking of her, and that he'd eschewed the lovey-dovey mood he'd wallowed in up at the Towsery earlier, having read the inspired, Human-penned 'Cat sat on the mat' poem. It made him think again of the student Humans.

I wonder if cats and Humans could ever communicate with each other? he thought. He put the thought to Biblio Chat, who merely looked indifferent. He cast his mind back to the male Human at the foyer who believed that he was trying to talk in 'cat' but was in fact just making purring meowing sounds. It suddenly occurred to him. *Maybe the Humans think we cannot speak, whereas in fact we can, but just choose not to?*

Biblio Chat looked up from his food, momentarily interested. He had once written to Library Cat:

For eons the Humans have thought we cannot talk. But they have also killed us believing us to be in cahoots with the devil during The Black Death, whereas the whole time we were feasting upon the very rodents that spread it. They have thought us lucky, then unlucky; eternally wise and couch-dwelling fools; hailed as gods in ancient Egypt and robbed of all dignity in the internet memes of the twenty-first century. Does it really surprise you to discover they think we cannot speak just because we chose not to in front of them? Us thinking cats have our own way of speaking, and its language glistens more than the sunniest sea they have ever beheld, and is just as rich and deep. We know the secrets of Babylon; the truths of the Orient, and all the beauties and ills of every continent on Earth. We are God in Paradise Lost *– understated and calm. Us thinking cats, we live for knowledge; it is its own end. The Humans, however, smother it beneath their personal desires for fame, money, sex and war. They covet knowledge like gold bullion putting a price on it at universities or shaming it to make killing machines. They are like the Devil in* Paradise Lost *– ever-moving, clanging and loud.*

And yet they insist we are the arrogant ones!

Biblio Chat's words hit Library Cat's tender mood hard. He knew these things, of course, but that didn't stave off his sudden worry for the safety of Humans and especially student-kind. His cousin continued…

But to answer your query, dear cousin: the Humans think we remain silent because we are mute. In fact, we remain silent because we are taciturn. Their philosopher Derrida explains this perfectly clearly – they need to pay more attention.

Library Cat bit his cat biscuit fiercely, his haunches high and his front legs lowered to his food bowl. He thought back to the girl on the phone, and the words she used when she spoke. He thought about other conversations he'd overheard, about the Humans' desires for each other, as well as things they craved and lamented regularly that they didn't have. Biblio Chat was right. It seemed that the Humans were forever comparing themselves to each other, or looking at points in the future or the past, or attempting acquisition of something, and feeling that their "present moment" fell short. It was true; knowledge did seem to be subjugated beneath the Humans' sleepless quest for personal gain.

He wandered away from his food bowl and over to his bed. The radiator behind it was warm, and before settling, he kneaded the sheepskin blanket into just the right shape. As the clock upstairs in the chaplaincy began striking midnight, everything became silent. All but Biblio Chat's soft purr filled the air as he remained up, sniffing the pages of several books, and rolling his head in catnip.

Then, just as Library Cat was dozing off to sleep, it hit him. *Contentment! That's what the Humans all *really* crave. That's what us cats have and they don't! It's not wealth, fortune, sex and fame that they need, just contentment. And the tragedy is not that they cannot achieve it but rather they don't know that it is contentment that they are craving. They always assume it's something else… another thing that needs to be achieved, or bought, or done… yet they've lost sight of the end goal. They make happiness an invisible mouse and then spend their entire life chasing it. But they just want contentment. There is no mouse to chase.*

Library Cat's head became heavy. It was all too much thinking for one day. He rested his head down on his sheepskin, and started counting sheep. *One, and indeed,*

Two; and, indeed, Three, and… And then the rest was sleep, and the deep silk of lovely dreams.

❖ Recommended Reading

More Fool Me by Stephen Fry.

❖ Food consumed

Piece of ham sandwich.

❖ Mood

Slightly concerned. Exhausted.

❖ Discovery about Humans

They have forgotten what it is they're running after.

Fireworks Night

*...in which our hero
narrowly avoids becoming enflamed*

Library Cat rose, after a long paw-twitching sleep. He stood on his hind legs upon the windowsill of his bedroom to survey the weather outside. Autumn was turning to winter and things seemed sharp. Instead of autumnal oranges and browns, the square was slowly becoming blanched of its colour. All seemed frigid and still. Without further ado, Library Cat headed out through his cat flap and trotted up the stone steps of the chaplaincy into the square, tiny little clouds once again gusting out of his mouth in the cold. It felt nice to leave Biblio Chat behind snoozing on the couch, and Library Cat's free, empty mind lifted up into the still air in a kind of relief. No more thinking. Not for today. Today was for a walk and exploring. The mousing season was nearly over, and Library Cat knew there'd be precious few remaining opportunities for a hunt. He sniffed the cold iron of the square's gates and glanced momentarily over to his right and to the yellow warmth of the library.

Winter is better lived in; but summer is better dreamed of, he mused suddenly, squeezing between the bars of the gate and into the peaceful greenery.

He hadn't walked any further than a couple of steps, and his mind hadn't done much more than congratulate itself for coming up with the insightful winter/summer maxim, than his paw knocked against something hard. He glanced down. Beneath his legs was a long stick, with what appeared to be a red mouse on the end of it. He assumed it was a mouse, since it was mouse-sized and had a long thin tail projecting from its rear. He craned his neck down to sniff it. It smelt spicy and fierce.

That is not a mouse! he thought, his heart pounding as he galloping a few paces back, the peppery odour still clinging to his nostrils. It smelt a bit like catnip and fire mixed

together. Tentatively he edged forward and re-examined the stick that seemed to impale the fiery-smelling mouse. He licked the end and gagged slightly. It was coloured red with yellow stripes. Nearby there was a soggy poster; it had the same red and yellow stripes plastered on it, top to bottom, and in the middle was large ballooning writing:

COME TO OUR FIREWORKS DISPLAY!!

THIS THURSDAY, 5TH NOVEMBER ON THE MEADOWS!

ALL WELCOME!! MISS IT AND MISS OUT!!!

Library Cat didn't like the poster. The plethora of exclamation marks alone made him deeply weary.

I'd rather miss out, he thought, sardonically going back to give the strange plastic mouse thing another sniff. Again he jumped, his eyes widening. There was something about the smell that spelt: fear-fear-fear!

I must get to the bottom of this business, he asserted to himself, and marched over to the bustling steps of the library.

The foyer of the library was pleasingly empty that afternoon. Library Cat slipped his head under the sliding glass gates and over to his favourite turquoise chair where he sat and pondered about how best to conduct his research on the red mouse-like stick thing. The odd student walked moodily up the zigzagging staircase, while in the far corner a Human in a yellow jacket started to push a large, droning box with a wet rotating disc under it for no apparent reason whatsoever. Library Cat watched it with suspicion, recalling his inexorable hatred of vacuum cleaners.

This is no place to think, he mused begrudgingly and with that he slipped away over to the secret portal to the Towsery.

That morning, the Towsery was alive with noise and commotion. Cats paced up and down agitated and mewing frantically, oblivious to the glow of the warm fire and the small platter of meats and milk that sat aside the fire grate. They eyed Library Cat's arrival furtively. There was an odd atmosphere in the air; the cats were anxious about something. It wasn't long before Library Cat deduced what all the fuss was about.

There, on the floor covered in hairs, was another of the mouseoid rocket things with a stick attached to it laying in the middle of the room, positioned carefully upon a small pile of books as if it were an exhibit in a crime case, or the biggest most bejewelled crown in the Tower of London. Next to it, several calendars were scattered, one of which was open at 5th November. Alongside these were history books, some old with golden-edged pages, and others newer with coloured illustrations. Library Cat looked upon these pictures with some alarm. Upon one of them was a sketch of a Human with a great beard donning a peculiar set of clothes entitled "Guy Fawkes". Across his jovial, belligerent face ran five parallel lashes where a cat's wrath had got the better of him, leading him to scratch the image of this Fawkes character and the shady threatening context that seemed to surround him. At the top left of the page there was printed in tiny, block capitals a date, 1605, and this had plainly caused some interest among the more learned thinking cats in the Towsery that morning, since many of the adjacent older books were opened at pages that also displayed 1605 alongside various articles and historical entries. Several notebooks lay nearby containing notes that the cats had evidently written out in haste.

As Library Cat began poring over the documents, it soon became clear that the Humans engaged in a type of ritualistic behaviour on 5th November. Things were burnt and detonated and they all bayed and swooned at the marvel of it all. It seemed that on this particular day, the Humans adopted rather backward behaviour that aligned itself closely with the bloodthirsty, torturous victimisation cats prior to the Enlightenment. Library Cat's eyes widened; he, like all thinking cats, was well versed since kittenhood in the Humans' cruel treatment of cats before the Enlightenment. Bad harvests, bad weather and tyrannical monarchs were just a couple of the things that featured within the inexhaustible list of Bad Things for which cats were wrongly accused. All because they apparently were the Devil's disciples. These days, the majority of Humans were educated and had eschewed these barbaric superstitions.

Towsers and cats that lived near libraries were especially immune. However, there were occasionally exceptions, and black cats or part-black cats like Library Cat were listed in the "Most-Likely-To-Be-Sacrificed-For-Witchcraft" category. Even some academic Humans had upheld their prejudices against the cat despite the Enlightenment. Good academic Humans too: Charles Bukowski, for instance, maintained up until his death that, "The cat is the beautiful devil."

Library Cat's eyes swivelled from article to article, his heartbeat increasing until they eventually rested upon one article in particular. On the top left of the page was a small column that had been violently underlined in red by the other cats:

On occasion, in Scotland and Edinburgh especially, similar acts of […] burning and torture were levelled against cats who were believed to be associated with the Jacobite line.
(39 qtd. in *The Thinking Cats' Guide to Existential Emergencies*)

Alongside the quotation was an image of an unfortunate cat in the grip of occultist Humans that Library Cat tried to forget. He stared into the middle distance, and took a deep breath:

OK. It's Bonfire Night. Stay calm, Library Cat, stay calm. Notice the article is written in the <u>past</u> tense. These things are OVER. Most Humans are, and will remain, Enlightened and will behave kindly towards cats. These mouse rocket things –

Fireworks – are so shaped to lure the more hapless, gullible cats into the Humans' ritualistic behaviours. But we are one step ahead of them. We know their game. We shall resist. We must all have faith that their sanity will return by morning.

Library Cat promptly set to work. From the back of his mind came the image of a particular book. He knew it was stored in the Towsery, and could identify it by its own unique scent-code within the dusty stacks. He speedily found it along the stack and prodded it with his paw so it plopped into the aisle the other side. He pawed it over to the group in the centre of the room.

Surviving Bonfire Night by F. H. Pushkin was a tried and tested survival guide for Bonfire Night whose instructions had been perfected and tweaked across the years in subsequent editions. Library Cat opened it to a double-page spread depicting an incredibly detailed schematic, replete with illustrations and arrows and peppered with bullet points. Along the top, in large letters, read the following:

THE THINKING CAT'S GUIDE TO SURVIVING FIREWORK NIGHT

- **STAY CALM.** The cat community is not under siege.
- **RESIST TEMPTATION** to eschew Humans. They cannot be blamed for their inferior hearing and warped sense of fun.
- **ABSTAIN FROM CATNIP.** Hallucinations can result, and this might cause chasing so-called "sparklers".

- **MAINTAIN DIGNITY** at all times. If your Human is kindly in nature, it is probable that they will subject you to a twenty-four-hour incarceration. Trust them. Maintain poise and refrain from chewing, spraying or soiling as this might result in your being jettisoned out into the hellish maelstrom.
- **REFRAIN FROM PURRING.** Try to cause your Human some mild concern by remaining close-at-hand, yet not quite yourself. This can also be affected by adopting the demeanour of existential malaise (see Camus, Baudelaire et al.) Know above all that the episode will pass and normality will resume.

Library Cat looked around at the panic. There were some cats he'd never seen before, whereas others he was sure he had seen but was pretty sure they were indoor cats, and had stolen away purely to attend this emergency meeting. This seemed to make them doubly nervous. As head Towser at Edinburgh University's Library, Library Cat felt he should do something to restore order. He let out a long, sonorous meow.

"Mmmmmmwwwwwwwwoooooooooohhhhhhrrrrr wwwww."

All of a sudden, the cats froze, their backs arched and their fur still spiky with tension. *That did the trick*, thought Library Cat to himself contentedly.

Suddenly, inches from one of the Towsery's high

windows, a shocking pink light flashed. All the Towsery's walls illuminated with bright stroboscopic light. Then blue then green then yellow. And finally, a few split seconds later, a series of enormous bangs. Suddenly, panic descended once again as if Library Cat's authoritative "meow" had merely paused them in a freeze-frame. This time, it was a while before Library Cat could restore order once more. *The first rockets are always the worst*, recalled Library Cat, the horror of former years now starting to come back to him.

The hours that followed were tense, but Library Cat kept order. The cats slowly started to calm down and have faith in Library Cat's reassurance. As night fell darker and darker, each cat chose an existential philosopher and read their work voraciously. By 9 pm, all cats were starting to feel confident that they could adopt a manipulative lustre of blame and anger that they could then direct towards their Human owners throughout the night, so that the latter might be guilt-tripped into thinking that their pet believed them to be completely and utterly responsible for all their suffering.

Eventually, Library Cat managed to convince the rest of the Towsers that enough Baudelaire and Sartre had been read, and that it was now time to put what they had learnt into practice and head home for incarceration.

Library Cat's walk back from the library to the chaplaincy that evening was unpleasant to be sure. The Humans had clearly run mad. In the square, some were lighting the tails of the so-called 'firework' mice and standing back as the object propelled itself into the stratosphere with a hellish squeak before eviscerating its insides in a great psychedelic balloon of fire and colour. A tangy miasma sat thickly upon the cold air, while down on the Meadows, just the other side of the library, a large bonfire had been lit. On it, the Humans had indeed place an effigy of Guy Fawkes. The flames that licked up around the sappy wood whistled in the breeze. There were whoops of joy and more bangs.

Well at least they seem to be having fun, thought Library Cat, upping his pace to the warm chaplaincy.

Inside, Biblio Chat was still sleeping peacefully on the couch and, as Library Cat curled up in his bed, the door of his basement room was promptly locked behind him.

I never did catch any mice, thought Library Cat sullenly as he dozed off to sleep, the bangs and pops slowly muting with the veil of night.

❧ Recommended Reading

Fireworks: Nine Profane Pieces by Angela Carter.

❧ Food consumed

2mg of gunpowder (later sicked up).

❧ Mood

Ambassadorial, poised.

❧ Discovery about Humans

Flashing lights and celebrations seem to make them happy.

"There, there, Library Cat!"

*...in which our hero
meets The Green Human*

The next morning, Library Cat was awoken with a rumble of the tummy. Hunger. Last night's commotion had left him feeling edgy and wide-eyed, but now his stomach was singing whale music to get his attention. He rolled over and over in his bed to try and settle it. The need to rise for food fell just short of a greater need to sleep more. From upstairs there came the sound of running water and the *scrub-a-dub-dub* sound of a Human thoroughly cleansing their nether regions.

Why must they make such a poppy show of it? thought Library Cat burying his head under his blanket from the noise. *And why are they up so early anyhow?*

He sank his head deeper under his blanket, but that was a little bit too hot. He rose and kneaded his blanket and turned a few times on the spot and attempted to settle again, but that was too cold. He picked up his blanket and dragged it into the room and away from the radiator, but there was a slight draft across his face. He buried his head once more, this time into his paws, and curled up tightly like an ammonite shell and tried his old tactic of counting sheep.

One, and indeed, Two, and indeed Three, and indeed, Four, and indeed, Five, and indeed, Six, and indeed…

All of a sudden from upstairs came the bellowing voice of a Human, muffled through the floorboards above.

"Library Cat? Oh, Library Cat? Where are you? It's OK, there's nothing to be scared of Library Cat…!"

Fine! thought Library Cat, opening his eyes and surrendering himself to the day. Sluggishly he rose and stretched, uttering a little "prrrrrp" with all the effort. Nosing out from his blanket, he sniffed the crumb-ridden carpet for a few morsels of cat food that had been scattered there. He followed this up by snapping at a couple of non-existent insects in the air above him. His tummy made a rumble once again.

"Library Cat! It's OK, you'll be all right, Library Cat!"

Waaaaaaaaaait a minute… thought Library Cat, his pupils suddenly dilating. *What do you mean "I'll be all right"? What are you planning to do to me?!* Something was awry: the Human was plotting. Up early, shower, pacing around looking for him while offering faux-reassurance in a disingenuously lilting voice? Something was wrong. Library Cat thought quickly. With the stealth of a panther, he slinked up the stairs into the hallway of the chaplaincy and into the living room. He could see the silhouette of the Human in the kitchen beyond, crouched down hunting for him behind the boiler.

Annnd… Distraction! thought Library Cat, biffing over a large vase with his paw sending it plummeting to an unearthly crash on the flagstones beneath, before bolting back down to his basement room for a post-match paw lick and scratch. Above he could hear his Human voicing yells of anger and incredulity.

That'll see him busy for the next twenty minutes, asserted Library Cat to himself contentedly.

In the calm that settled, Library Cat began to prepare for the day. He soon became acutely aware of a most glorious smell. His mouth began to water. Following his nose, he found his way to the cat flap. There, spread out on the laundry room floor, was the most delicious hamper of freshly slayed prey he had ever beheld. It teemed with blues, browns, greys and violets... all the variety a cat could ever want. Firstly, beneath his forepaws, was a stout trout recently caught from Duddingston Loch. It glimmered green and silver in the midday sun. Then there was a prime Grassmarket rat, long of tail and plump of belly. Beneath this lay an Arthur's Seat rabbit, muscular of leg and pert of ear. And finally there was a spectacular Pentland Pheasant, her rainbow feathers perfectly interlaced, and her downy breast succulent. All this was topped off with a side of assorted beetle, woodlouse and grasshopper.

Next to the dazzling array was a note:

Cher cousin,
Pour l'hiver...
Adieu,
Biblio Chat

How on earth does he do it? Library Cat thought to himself, open-mouthed with awe at the breath-taking finesse with which his cousin caught, prepared and arranged the food. The hunting ability alone was something Library Cat could only marvel at, forcing him to bow down at the altar of true and timeless art.

Voraciously, Library Cat tucked in until his hunger and the drama of the day before was little more than a memory. Happily he purred, smacked his lips, and thought about how he could never think ill of his cousin again, and that he must write to him and say "je suis désolé" and invite him back again, until he finally dozed off for a delicious mid-morning nap fatefully forgetting all about the Human's peculiar behaviour earlier and the broken vase.

The next thing Library Cat knew he was in a box. A grilled door had slammed shut and he was being carried. *I must've been cornered in the laundry room!* The box lumbered haphazardly with the gait and enormous strides of the Human carrying it, and Library Cat felt as if he were a cormorant riding the great waves of an Atlantic storm. Now he was outside and in one of the great machines that regularly parked along the perimeters of the square as it whirred and clanged, and seemed to speed up, faster and faster... When it was moving, it vibrated like a washing machine, and when it was still, it purred softly like a great cat. Sometimes, when it was still, Library Cat managed to peer through the grilled box door at his Human who was just ahead of him. The Human sat drumming his fingers on a big circular wheel as if waiting for something, while a little velvety *click-click-click-click* sounded in unison with a tiny green arrow that flashed either left or right in a panel behind a great wheel. Then, all would be a fury of motion again, and the machine would turn a sharp corner forcing Library Cat to raise his paw perpendicular to himself in order that he might save himself rolling over and over, like a speck of dirt in a cyclone-separator or a ball in a raffle machine.

Stop! Stop! Stop! thought Library Cat. But his thoughts licked like silent red flames through his head; a tiny brain-box, inside his carrying-box, which was inside the big Human machine-box. A Russian doll of boxes. And Library Cat's screaming brain was like the smallest doll in the very centre – hidden, yet blaring with the colour and symbolism of a million pogroms.

Maybe I'm going to London? speculated Library Cat suddenly as he recalled Saaf Landan Tom's description of something called "The London Underground". Apparently, where Tom lived, there were large buildings that smelt of shoe polish and inside them there were things called escalators – great, endlessly lapping tongues of steel – that carried the Humans deep underground into a stomach of sinister noises and smells. A veritable cat hell. And if that wasn't enough, the Humans then packed themselves, often thousands of them in one go, onto these long, narrow pieces of concrete called "platforms" that were only a few feet wide while awaiting the arrival of a massive, terrifying piston to scream towards them, plunging a fug of filthy air into their eyes. They would then climb into the piston, and disappear to another shoe-polishy-smelling building where they would re-emerge. Saaf Landan Tom's description had haunted Library Cat ever since.

"This torture-prison… How long do they remain there? Until they confess their crime?" Library Cat had asked.

"Nah, nah, nah, nah mate… The 'umans go dahn there outa choice."

"Choice?!"

"Yeah, mate. They go dahn there to get uva places in Landan, innit."

"Other places?"

"Yeah."

"But, why?"

"Coz loadza people liv' in Landan. The roads are too full so they 'av to move people abaht unda' the ground."

"But we have plenty of space up here. Why do they cram themselves in down there?"

"Sumfin' called 'The Economy'."

"What's that?"

"Dunno."

"Well it must be great, whatever it is, to make all those horrors worthwhile. Tell me, Tom, do the Humans live especially well in London? I assume they have plenty of time to read, muse, eat and relax to make up for this 'Underground' torture?"

"Nah. The opposite, mate. My last owna' paid £600 a monf, to live under some stairs, and eats only sumfin' called 'pasta'."

"Then can we agree, Tom, that this is the definitive proof of the insanity of Humankind?"

"Totally, mate."

Library Cat sniffed the air. As far as he could tell he couldn't pick up any traces of shoe polish.

So long as it's not London, I should be fine, thought Library Cat.

Eventually, the noisy box slowed, reversed slightly, and then came to a standstill. Soon Library Cat felt himself being hoisted out. The Weetabixy smell of Edinburgh hit his nostrils once more and he felt calmer. He was still in the same city. Through the slatted mesh of his box he could see Humans everywhere, but they didn't look like students. Instead they walked quickly, and wore impressive clothes. The ladies had button-noses and grouted faces, and the men had shiny, ebony-coloured shoes and suits. Beneath his box, Library Cat saw the gum-freckled pavement flash past, along with bright coloured sweet wrappers and cardboard cups. Now the air was thick with the braided din of sirens and buses, interspersed with the odd "Ding! – Ding! – Ding!" as a long snake-like vehicle on rails glided across the road as if by magic.

Seems perfectly horrendous. Maybe I am in London? postulated Library Cat to himself as his owner rounded a corner and pushed open a door.

Suddenly there was a waft of antiseptic and the squelchy sound of rubber floors. Library Cat froze.

The Vet!!! The Vet!!!

Library Cat cried, and began writhing like a snared fox. His Human raised him up and stared in through the gauze at his face.

"There, there, Library Cat!"

Don't you "there-there" me, you ***!@^&$%!** TRAITOR!! LET ME OUT NOW! Not here, not here, not here. PLEASE NOT HERE. Anywhere BUT HERE! Traitor, YOU BLASTED TRAITOR! Bath, The Rain, The Black Dog, Collars, Fireworks… London. Anything BUT HERE! You said NEVER AGAIN. DAMN YOU, HUMAN! You ************ TRAITOR, DAMN YOU.

"Library Cat, calm yourself! It will be OK!"

"Sir, would you like to place Library Cat on the table? Do you want to be present for the procedure?"

Not The Green Human, not The Green Human!

"Er, yes, I'll stay and talk to him, if that's OK. Um… any chance of a cup of tea?"

CUP OF TEA? Who do you think you are, the Queen of Sheba, you TRAITOR, you…

"Of course, black or white, sir?"

"Um, black please?"

Huh, yeah!! Black: the colour of your SOUL, treacherous Human!! Doesn't surprise me Human…!

"OK. Karen, would you get the gentleman a black tea?"

Yes, feel free to spike it from ME, Karen!

"Right just pop his box on the table. How long did you say he's been suffering for?"

About ten minutes now, you cretins?

"Um… about two weeks?"

Two Weeks? Do you live in a world of fiction…?!

"OK, it's quite a simple procedure. The X-ray shows there's three stones in his bladder, but there might be a couple more now. They often form during periods of anxiety. Did you keep him in on fireworks night?"

Err… yes I was INCARCERATED, since you must know…

"Yes I did, he seemed fine, but he was in a fight a couple of weeks ago…"

"Ah OK, it could very well be that. Oh come, come, none of that hissing, Library Cat! I think we might need to calm you down! (I think we better give him a shot first just to settle his nerves)."

Um… I think NOT, you slithering bolus of snakes…

"OK, if you think that's best."

And what about what I think?!

Library Cat felt the door of his box swing open and the fingers of The Green Human clench around the scruff of his neck. Then he felt the fur by his waist being pinched thickly and firmly as if it were caught in a door. His whiskers trembled. Resisting, he mustered all his strength to drag himself along the table. A thin film of sweat had coated the underside of his paws, and the table was plastic and slippery. As a result, Library Cat's paws skidded across it as if it were an icy paving slab white with a winter hoarfrost. And then Library Cat's mind blacked out… numbed into darkness by pain and the smell of antiseptic.

The next thing he knew, all thoughts had ceased. In one corner, he saw a screen with green worms on it that writhed rhythmically to the sound of "bibb-bibb-bibb-bibb". In the other corner, he saw a second Green Human preparing a strange mixture. Normally, at times like this, Library Cat would devise a plot – a manipulation, a machination, but whenever he attempted to engage his brain in the grip of the Green Human, his mind yelled back in a long, spiralling loop of nouns, strung together like a summer bunting: *pain!-SURVIVAL-pain!-SURVIVAL-pain!-SURVIVAL-pain!-SURVIVAL-pain!-SURVIVAL-pain!-SURVIVAL-pain!-SURVIVAL-pain!*

Library Cat's eyes blurred as he saw the second Green Human pour the strange mixture into a thing that vaguely resembled a mouse with a long, straight and extremely sharp tail. He watched the last drop bungee from the end of the container like honey from a spoon. Then they inverted the mouse thing, and pushed the end, sending a little spurt of liquid high into the air.

"You feeling better, Library Cat?"

"M-wah," said Library Cat weakly, his eyes half closed.

Now the first Green Human tightened their grip as the second Green Human walked purposely towards him and then disappeared beyond him. The last thing Library Cat remembered was the pain of a red-hot, sharp fang pushing thickly into his ruched-up fur.

Silence.

"Library Cat! Can you hear me?"

I can indeed, thought Library Cat.

"Look, a treat! You've been such a good boy!"

Kindly don't patronise me. I've been no different to usual. Where am I?

Library Cat looked around him. He was in a waiting room, but was unsure why. Gradually the neurons in his brain started to warm up and flicker with memories, like a cantankerous photocopier receiving its first user of the day. *The vet. The Green Human. The gratuitous and sudden cruelty.* Tentatively he stood up. He saw, in front of him, a parcel of blooded dressing. Looking at it made him feel suddenly light and faint like a delicate papier-mâché lampshade. Then he remembered. He sat down again. Numerous Humans were stroking him gently. He heard himself purr. This shocked him, because the moment he heard himself purr, he knew that he couldn't conceal his hostility any longer. He felt relaxed, and grateful for the Humans' company. A pressure had been released somewhere near his rear end. Gradually he lifted himself upon all four paws once again. The Humans fell suddenly, respectfully quiet as if half-expecting him to break into an exemplary recital of Rimsky-Korsakov's 'Flight of the Bumblebee' at the pianoforte. He edged to the side of the table and leapt off.

"M-wahhhh!"

Library Cat had landed with a splat on the floor, all four paws splayed outwards like tent poles, and his aerial image resembling the flayed skin of a Scottish Wildcat, pinned barbarically upon the living room of some nobleman's mansion.

"Too much too soon, Library Cat," the Green Human said between laughs. "He'll be a bit woozy for the next hours. Make sure he remains hydrated, and refrain from giving him salty treats for the next forty-eight hours. Oh and ensure he keeps the cone on."

Cone? What cone? Why are you talking about a cone? mused Library Cat, mildly perturbed.

And then he noticed. Cutting in along the radius of his peripheral vision was a large plastic circle.

The Cone of Shame! wept Library Cat inwardly as he envisaged how ridiculous he must look with an enormous satellite dish for a head.

If they wanted me to not scratch, they've only to ask politely. Oh not the Cone of Shame. Anything but the Cone of Shame!

Later that day Library Cat began feeling his way around the chaplaincy with a massive plastic cone on his head obscuring his view and mocking his spatial awareness. He tried to conceal his humiliation by hiding in the gap between the fridge and the boiler. It was one of his favourite spaces. But the Cone of Shame stopped him. He tried diverting his sorrow by riffling through books, but the Cone of Shame snagged the pages. He tried eating, but the Cone of Shame scooped up his biscuits and flung them in the air. Giving up and feeling sorry for himself, he decided to go for a walk... but the Cone of Shame snagged on the cat flap. Finally, he discovered that the Cone of Shame was much like the barb on a fishing line, and that if he reversed into the necessary spaces, he could get himself into them. So he reversed out the cat flap, reversed through the railings of George Square, and reversed through the glass gates of the library, and up into the stairs to the Towsery.

Sheepishly, Library Cat skulked along the rafters to the Towsery where the warmth of the fire was already circling down the cone and onto his fur. *The Head Towser of Edinburgh University Library! Wearing the Cone of Shame. Oh the Humiliation.*

As he turned the corner to this evenings gaggle of thinking cats – all either high-tailed among the stacks, nibbling at mice between the rafters, or flicking through ancient tomes by the orange firelight – Library Cat paused, awaiting the inevitable rumble of jeering purrs. Indeed they came, but subsided quickly also. After all, most cats face the Cone of Shame at some point in their lives, and while especially humiliating for a thinking cat, it never need stand in the way of a cat's character. Promptly the other Towsers jumped up and set to work nibbling the tight meshed plastic around Library Cat's neck. Library Cat was moved at the sudden act of camaraderie, and felt his humiliation begin to dissolve.

Eventually he was free, and he stretched with plentiful purrs of gratitude, nuzzling the faces of his faithful saviours.

Later, Library Cat headed back to the chaplaincy. He knew that at some point he'd have to confront his Human again. A bubble of panic curdled in his belly. He wondered whether he could trust his Human any more after he'd taken him along to the Vet without asking his permission. He went into his room and hid.

"Library Cat? Oh, Library Cat, come out from under there! All right, all right, I'll take off my green coat. There. Happy now? Oh Library Cat, please come out from under there. It's OKAY, Library Cat, trust me. Ahhh… There! You see? I told you…"

Mmm, good stroke.

"I'm sorry you had to go through that earlier, Library Cat. But it was for your own good."

Please don't bring up the Green Human. I'll forgive you in time.

"Don't give me that look, it was for your own good, Library Cat. Trust me."

Trust you? Mmmm… agreeable ear-tickle… mmm…

"There, there. Oh no, Library Cat, what have you done with your Cone?"

Run!

Library Cat bolted between the fridge and the boiler. As the evening drew on, he gave himself a good preen. He was sweaty and matted, and it does a thinking cat's pride no good when he or she looks like they've been dragged up from the Union Canal. He thought about the day with delicious detachment.

I guess when someone says things aren't right, you have to trust them, even if it does hurt, and everyone around you does seem mad, he thought, as he crossed his paws and dozed with the warm, blue glow of the boiler flickering next to him.

❧ Recommended Reading

'Ambulances' by Philip Larkin.

❧ Food consumed

1 cat treat, 2 tiny bits of plastic (from Cone of Shame).

❧ Mood

Fearful (morning), humiliated (early afternoon), touched (early evening), emboldened (late evening).

❧ Discovery about Humans

They sometimes shield the truth for fear of being judged.

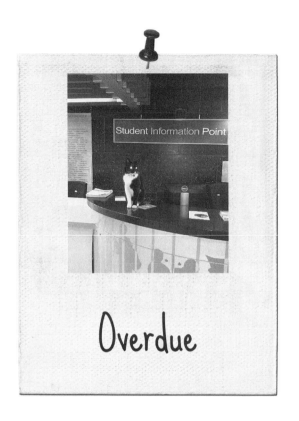

Overdue

…in which our hero
discovers the meaning of the word "fine"

Several days had passed since Library Cat chewed himself free of the Cone of Shame, and he had settled quite comfortably back into his usual routine. Morning: rise at 9.30 am, doze for an hour. Mid-Morning: breakfast, head to turquoise chair for snooze. Early Afternoon: disappear to the Towsery for reading. Early evening: hunting, supper and bed.

This particular morning, Library Cat had roused from his slumber and spent a good half an hour simply admiring the piles of books in his bedroom in the chaplaincy. They scattered around him almost as far as the eye could see, and when his Human came down to change his food, he often took some time to negotiate carefully between the various piles, slurping his fresh bowl of water in the process. Some piles were only a couple of books deep, others towered haphazardly up like a three-year-old's early attempts at civil engineering, and seen together at their various heights, they seemed to resemble the dancing bars of a graphics equaliser on a nineties stereo system, each one a different colour and height, shimmying up and down as if to some hidden symphony of knowledge.

I really should sort through them, thought Library Cat, yawning.

Although Library Cat conducted most of his reading in the Towsery itself (if nothing else, the Towsery was a constant source of warmth), there was sometimes nothing better than smelling a book, sitting with a book, and – indeed – reading a book in the comfort of your own bed. The street lamp from the square would glimmer in through the window, and by his radiator-heated sleeping and reading station, Library Cat could devour several books in one evening, purring dulcetly over the half-lit pages in sublime pleasure. And so, by a certain magic stealth, Library Cat had obtained transit of numerous books from the library back to his own bedroom. Over the years their numbers increased as his reading tastes diversified, leading him to forget how long he'd had each one of them. Little did he grieve over the countless students who were, the whole time, being wrongly accused of stealing library books after he had intercepted them halfway along the Returns conveyor belt, biffing them off with his pernicious paw. Indeed, when he settled down to *The Cambridge Companion to Charles Dickens* of an evening, he hardly twitched a whisker at the thought that Matriculation Number S0791986 had been frozen and attached with several stratospheric fines, and that a High Court Order had been issued against a certain Mr Andrew Butterfield of Flat 2/2 Marchmont Crescent, who spent evenings pacing his room with trembling hands, and whose friends said he'd "developed a persecution complex of late". No. Library Cat was blissfully ignorant of such things, and nor is it in the nature of a thinking cat – nor any cat for that matter – to spend valuable reading and sleeping time delving into the minutiae of a library's lending policy.

There were some books in his bedroom that belonged to his Human, that was for sure... both Library Cat and his Human possessed a shared interest in the Palladian landscape revival of the early Pre-Raphaelite period. But most of them belonged to the library. The ones that belonged to the library, however, were very easy to identify. They were the ones with little stickers on their spines that displayed a series of numbers and letters. These formed around 90 per cent of the pile, and also bore the crest of Edinburgh University emblazoned on their colophon page.

I suppose I should return them some day, ruminated Library Cat. *But then again*, he thought, *they are very big books. And the library is surely aware that such books will require some time to finish reading, and more time still to study properly. Take this book for instance – the one that has "HUB RESERVE" written on its spine. It's called* Marxism and Literary Criticism *by a Human called Terry Eagleton. That is an enormous topic, and no doubt numerous scholars and thinking cats have devoted their entire lives to studying Marxism in literature alone. I mean, it's not as if I could feasibly read* Marxism and Literary Criticism *in – say – three hours, is it? That would be utterly ridiculous.*

And so Library Cat, confident in his conjectures, and putting off the return of his books for another week, or month, or year, rose from his bed, walked over to an open book, and sat on it as a throne upon which to commence his morning preening regime. Once completed, he sneezed on another book that had "SPECIAL ARTEFACT" written on its spine, sicked up a fur ball on another that had "HANDLE ONLY WITH GLOVES" on its side, and finally sharpened his paws on the papyrus-like ancient pages of a third book stating "DO NOT REMOVE FROM LIBRARY". He gazed down at the gouges made in the yellowing paper in the wake of his paws.

This completed, he finally tucked into a breakfast of

woodlice and catnip. Presently, it was reading time and Library Cat nosed his way towards the cat flap that already swung open and closed in the wind.

The air outside was glacial. Everywhere, hands were shoved down pockets and necks were thickly embossed with coloured scarfs. Above, an aeroplane droned crisply through the air. Library Cat watched as it banked towards the Firth of Forth, and then left towards Edinburgh Airport, its landing gear lowering like a gently unfolding popup book.

Weird bird, he thought, eyeing it suspiciously as it disappeared from view, his pupils dilating with curiosity. *I must seek out its nest one day*.

Just as Library Cat began to ponder how a bird could fly so steadily, with no flap of the wings, and what such a bird's nest would look like and how best to hunt it, there came through the air the clap-clap-clap-clap sound of running shoes. Library Cat looked to his left. A student was darting along the perimeter of the square towards the library. In his left arm, he cradled a precarious stack of books; in his right he held a telephone up to his ear into which he yelled frantically.

"Yah, I, like, totally forgot I had two HUB Reserve books overnight, they're, like, hours overdue. I'm going to have a massive fine, and not be able to graduate until it's paid off, yah? They charge you £2 for each minute…?"

Hmmmm, thought Library Cat, his mind turning to the thousands of library books he kept in his bedroom. The image sat comfortably in his head for about two and a half seconds before a thick panic began to gloop through muscles like mantle. *A few hours overdue… and yet this Human seems very worried.*

Then it struck Library Cat like a rock. How could he have been so stupid?

A FINE!

And so it was, that at that very moment, Library Cat was introduced to that heinous mix of feelings that all stalwart-yet-tardy library users are familiar with: financial anxiety, shame, guilt and, of course, loneliness resulting from lifelong ostracism from the library in question. His name would be denounced. No more Towsery. No more bacon rind! No more warmth! A cat in the doghouse…

Every minute! Every MINUTE!? (Library Cat turned the word over and over in his head like a fluffy catnip ball.)

So I've been charged £2 for every minute The Complete Works of Friedrich Nietzsche *was not returned to the HUB Reserve? Dating back all the way to 30th October 2012? But that's… £4,261,120!* thought Library Cat, beads of sweat now beginning to seep through the underside of his paws and onto the clammy tarmac.

And that's just ONE BOOK! I have over 150 books out at present, so that's…(!)

Library Cat's mind folded in at the figure. He had nothing to compare it with. He'd once overheard that seventy-five million Humans had read his thoughts on the Internet, but this figure far exceeded that. It was a figure only comparable to those that astrophysicists use to describe the distance to the outermost satellite of the outermost planet orbiting the outermost star in the outermost solar system known to Humankind... stated in millimetres.

He thought fast.

Missing, I have to go missing!

Library Cat had always been reluctant to go missing. Biblio Chat often played the *Chat Perdu* card whenever he'd vomited on the carpet. Biblio Chat would then vainly admire the pictures of himself pasted up on the local boulangerie window, before clawing them down by the veil of night and storing them as valedictory talismans for his already hugely inflated ego. He'd then return home to cuddles and a veritable bounty of sweetmeats in his basket. All in all, it made the self-induced vomiting thoroughly worthwhile.

But to Library Cat, going missing always seemed like the coward's way out somehow – effective in garnering contrition among Humans, but never really resolving any issues. It'd be a short-term solution. He'd still be a cat on the run...

How can I pay up? I don't have any money! A bird perhaps?

Library Cat had attempted to offer his thanks by delivering a bird to the library staff once, but the act of generosity had dramatically backfired. Hearing the shrieks of disgust as he placed the bird at the feet of one particular librarian as she enjoyed a sandwich on her break, Library

Cat assumed that the bird was not satisfactory to her taste. Consequently he went back out on the hunt the next night and caught an even bigger bird as well as a rat. *This cannot fail to delight*, he'd thought, but the response the next day was even worse.

So I cannot get a bird. Umm… ummm… ummm…

Library Cat found himself pacing up and down on the spot. A lion locked in the cage of his own anxiety. Despite his books being overdue now for several years, and despite having never once been reprimanded or called to account over his crime, Library Cat nevertheless felt utterly sure that at this very moment, he was being watched by scores of surveillance computers, tracking his every move from space, each one poised to intervene at a moment's notice sending a gaggle of baying Humans looking for him. All this time he'd been at peace when he should've been fraught with worry! All this time he's been holding the gaze of myriad CCTV cameras, all latched onto him, swivelling sinisterly on their necks like a flock of malevolent barn owls. There were probably a host of computers all packed high with details of his book theft. By night, he was an infrared blob seen from above, a glowing tumour darting under bushes on the Meadows and George Square, seen even despite the thick, luminous alveoli that made up Edinburgh's patchwork of streets and cul-de-sacs when viewed from the night sky.

Purring. Surely I can just purr. Purring solves everything.

I shall purr all debts clean. It's scientifically proven to have a manipulative effect upon Humans.

With a game plan, Library Cat felt a little better. Convinced that ostracism from the library loomed ever closer, he took a deep breath and walked over to the library, ducked under the glass doors, and marched high of head and straight of tail over to the Help Desk counter.

"Evenin' Library Cat."

"Purr purr purr purr."

"Okay, Okay, I'll get ye some bacon… jus' wait there…"

Job's a good'un, thought Library Cat, *this seems to be going well.*

As he waited for the librarian to return with the promised bacon, the same student he'd seen running earlier with the books arrived at the counter next to him. He watched as he unloaded the ungainly stack of monographs on the desk in front while the librarian scanned them one by one. When the librarian reached the final book, she looked interrogatingly back at her computer screen.

"Honestly, that's, like all the books I have? I don't, like, have any more?"

"According to our records," the librarian said weightily, "we're still due back *The Complete Works of Friedrich Nietzsche…*"

A cold sweat ran through Library Cat down to his paws.

"No, I swear I returned that years ago, I swear."

"Hmmm."

Waaaaait a minute, thought Library Cat suddenly, a relief starting to tingle across his fur like a warm duvet. *The fine isn't mine at all. The fine belongs to the Human that the library THINKS has the books.*

Library Cat looked back at the student Human. His head was bowed in embarrassment, and the palms of his hands were ever-so-slightly sweaty.

Is this fair? Library Cat wondered to himself, with a sudden twinge of guilt. *Is it fair that this man is being punished in my place? Is it fair that I roam a free cat, and this Human goes to judgement in my stead?*

Suddenly the librarian turned towards Library Cat, her spectacles balanced at the end of a pointed, unyielding nose. Their eyes met, but that was enough. Library Cat could take no more. The pressure was too much. He took to his heels and galloped out of the library, and towards the Meadows park, his guilt two feet behind him at all times like an autumn wasp, just as the first librarian re-entered smiling with steaming hot crispy bacon.

❧ Recommended Reading

Les Misérables by Victor Hugo.

❧ Food consumed

Woodlice, catnip.

❧ Mood

Guilty, fearful.

❧ Discovery about Humans

Their rules take the pleasure out of things.

Missing

...in which our hero goes to Marchmont

Library Cat ran and ran in the pouring rain. His paws started to feel numb and cold as he galloped through watery clods of mud on the Meadows. As he ran, he looked over his shoulder at intervals towards the library. The mirage of its grey, square form bounced up and down through the drizzle with the motion of his run, getting further and further away by the second. To his left was the great hill of Arthur's Seat, shimmering uncannily in the fog as if superimposed there by a lazy special effects editor. He felt himself panting like a dog. Without stopping he darted across a main road. A car braked just in time. Had he been any slower, or had his coat possessed a little more black than light-reflecting white, or had he not stared in the direction of the car with eyes not quite as vibrant and neon green, things would almost certainly have turned out differently. Eventually he slowed his pace, his front legs beginning to buckle. Calming down, he headed up a small alley, called "Meadow Place Lane". Torrents of water poured out of gutters as a wind howled all around. Everywhere broken umbrellas lay in bins bent and twisted like electrocuted daddy longlegs. The air smelt dank with the fresh smell of moss and earth, which wasn't altogether unpleasant. Shortly he found himself in a square. A large tree stood in the centre of it, bejewelled with white Christmas lights. Behind it stood a shop called Scotmid.

I've heard talk of this fabled place, thought Library Cat gazing up at the large sign. He sauntered over and sat just shy of the threshold, feeling pleasant wafts of warm air slip out during the moments that Humans entered and left through an automatic door. He thought about the journey he'd just made in an effort to keep alive its various details for the return trip.

There was the library, the big park, the car, and then the… what came next?

But the harder he tried to recall the details, the faster they seemed to recede back from view, like a knowing mouse in its hole when it gets the whiff of hungry cat stalking slowly close by the other side.

"Hello, cat, you look lost."

Library Cat looked up. Above him was a bearded, gangly Human, quite possibly a student, carrying a large square box, from which he extracted and chewed large Trivial Pursuit segments of some doughy food. It smelt wonderfully of anchovies and tuna. Library Cat rubbed his side against the student, purring loudly, and was duly rewarded for his affection with a morsel of the stodgy anchovy goodness which dropped to his feet. It was the most delicious thing Library Cat had ever tasted. The Human started to move away.

Um, I think not, thought Library Cat, trotting after him, his tail held high in the air, as if the Human had suddenly morphed into the Pied Piper of cats. Presently, Human and cat turned a corner towards a large green door that opened into a stairwell.

"No, no, no, you can't come in here. Go home!"

I'll go home when I please, thought Library Cat, *but first I'm having more of that stodgy anchovy stuff. And I'm also not altogether sure where home is at the moment.*

The tenement stairwell was echoey. Beneath Library Cat's paws were small black and white square tiles as if its Human designers had entertained a funny notion that one day other Humans might be inclined to play chess there. Higher and higher they spiralled until Library Cat felt the warm waft from an open door. He darted in.

It was a student flat. In the room straight ahead of him a few Humans sat on the floor while drinking a clear fluid from tiny cups which seemed to them to be disproportionately funny. From another room to his left, a big black cloud wafted into the hallway as an unspeakably loud alarm started to squeak on the ceiling, while another Human balanced dubiously on a three-legged chair to try and whack said alarm with the end of a broom. And from yet another room, whose door was propped open rather randomly by a traffic cone, there came the noise of "grrrrr"s and "arrrrgh"s (and worse) as another student jabbed away at a laptop keyboard, illuminated exclusively by the dull glow of an adjacent desk lamp.

So this is how the other side live, thought Library Cat, following after the bearded Human and the delicious hammy stuff into the main room with the giggling drinkers.

"Guys, we've got a new flatmate."

"Eeeeeeeeeee! Oh my god he's so cute, can we keep him?"

Of course you can't, you moron, thought Library Cat.

"Oh my God, can you pick him up?" said another, hoisting Library Cat up by the belly so that his head and back end flopped pathetically downward like a damp rugby sock.

Kindly place me back down and leave me be.

"Aw, he's quite friendly."

Mmmmm… no I'm not.

"He doesn't seem to bite or claw…"

I have the power to, should I so wish.

"Careful, he's looking a bit grumpy. I'd put him down if I were you."

Yes, so would I "if I were you".

"Have you fed him?"

"Well he likes this pizza…"

"Make him some dinner."

Good thought…

"Here puss puss puss puss puss. Over HERE puss puss puss…"

Yes, I know. I'm not blind.

"Has he gottun a collar on?"

It's "has he got a collar on" not "has he 'gottun' a collar on".

"Um no don't think so…"

"Is he that cat that hangs out in George Square? What's he called… Library Cat?"

Honestly, you should really know who I am by now.

"Yeah it's HIM!"

Oh God, baulked Library Cat, squirming suddenly from a clammy grasp and bolting towards the kitchen.

Out in the kitchen, the smoke had slightly subdued and a window had been flung lavishly open, sending great rolling plumes of icy air into the room. Wary from the overabundance of attention he received in the living room,

Library Cat eavesdropped upon a conversation through a crack along the hinge of the door.

"He said, that she said, that he said, that he pulled her on a night out," a boy was saying to a girl.

"Really... no way."

"Yeah. And Tom said that Livvy said that Lawrence thinks that isn't true?"

"Right."

"But did he say to you anything about what she said to him?"

This conversation is unfathomable, flinched Library Cat, backing away from the door, wondering how it was possible for one sentence to have so many pronouns and not one antecedent. *That dark room seemed more my kind of room.* He made his way to the room with the single yellow light glowing over a desk and behind it a girl holding her head as if its contents might explode. The room was big and cold. An electric heater glowed in the corner, sending out the throat-rasping scent of burning dust. Christmas lights adorned the window, and a pin board hung, slightly skee-whiff, above the desk.

"This question just doesn't make any sense!" the girl suddenly piped up, rising from her chair and beginning to pace the room holding a scrunched piece of paper that she gazed at in fits and starts. Finally, with one massive sigh, she cast the paper down to the floor, sending it swirling on a little loop-the-loop and coming to rest by Library Cat's paws at the door. Then she plonked down on the bed in the darkness;

a few moments later her face glowed a dullish white from the screen of her mobile phone.

Library Cat looked at the paper. It contained a quotation and a question for an academic essay:

"Governmental power intrinsically; unleashes; energises; propagates and responds to a post-Romantic crisis of the 'self' in Foucault's writing." – D. Baxter

Substantiate; Authenticate; Exonerate or Repudiate Baxter's statement.

Library Cat felt sick.

No wonder she's confused. The professor is trying to intimidate her with the use of semicolons. Punctuation should communicate, not intimidate.

Feeling suddenly sad for the girl, Library Cat ventured in. He looked under the bed momentarily. Dust, single shoes and bus tickets lay variously scattered in its cavernous gloom, along with a single earring which Library Cat was sure the girl must've given up trying to find. He looked up at the girl. She sniffed and glided her finger along her phone's oblong cube of light. She seemed despondent. Library Cat felt moved by her evident despair. *Maybe I'll say hello?* He tiptoed silently along the foot of her bed.

"Meow?"

"What the F***!" said the girl scrambling to her feet in total shock, sending her phone smashing to the floor.

Library Cat took to his heels and darted out the door and up a small set of stairs into the eves of an attic, his chest pounding and his paws prickling with rushing blood. A few moments later his eyes adjusted to the light. He took a few steps forward, his tail swishing curtly. The attic seemed a little like the Towsery but felt much colder, and had a peculiar herby smell. Mould crept up one wall, blooming in various daubs of grey and green like a Seurat painting, while on the opposing wall, a layer of paint flaked off the side of a stone-cold gas boiler.

Strange pictures hung on the wall – some old oils of the Highlands in moulded gold frames that looked like heirlooms, others plainer and more abstract of Scottish tenements. Clothes hung mildewed on a drying rack, and the carpet beneath his paws felt wiry and scratchy. Above, a skylight window held the moon in a slightly oblique frame – its platinums and black-blues seeming mysterious. Sitting on top of the window was a scattered array of bottles and little lozenges and Library Cat wondered how on earth they got there.

He suddenly felt calmer. Despite its dampness, the attic had a nice feel to it. Excitement and mystery seemed to commingle in its very atmosphere. What's more, it was high up, and Library Cat enjoyed being high up. Sniffing along the corridor for mice, he heard a noise from a room. Walking over to the door in question, he paused for a minute, and pushed it with his paw. It swung open with a creek. A herby fug hit his nostrils. On a bed in the far corner, under the slope of the roof above, a boy lay on his bed in shorts, eyes half-closed smiling inanely as if in some sort of a trance.

"Duuuuuuuuuuuuuude", he said lazily.

Indeed? thought Library Cat.

"Hahaha Duuuude", the boy repeated again between laughs. "Duuude, how'd you get in, pussy cat?"

The Human's voice sounded strange – sort of sloweddown, like a cat's when initiating a fight. On the floor were many scraps of paper with countless bits of writing on them scrawled messily in an incredibly inelegant hand. Library Cat gazed closely at one of them:

The Meaning of Life: Discoveries while High

1 ... group ~~love, communism~~ WORLD ~~SEX~~ PEACE be happy [*illegible*]…
2…. Ireland is *an island!!!!!!*

Library Cat paused. *The Human is clearly a moron*, he thought turning to leave. *And charming as it is, this place is incredibly cold. It is no place for me to make my new life. They have books, I grant them, but their ways are too bizarre for me. This is their "down time" and yet they have found very odd ways of relaxing. I wonder if most Humans descend into madness behind closed doors?*

As Library Cat moved discreetly towards the stairs, something else struck him about the way in which the student Humans live. Up until now, he hadn't noticed the plethora of notes pinned up everywhere on various walls. Beneath the clothes horse in the hall, for instance, was one that said the following:

ATTENTION FLATMATES:

Throwing my stuff on the floor when it is not yet dry is *NOT OKAY!!!*

Wait til it's dry or use the other rack.

Cheers lovelies,

Tiff xx

Upon the door of the bedroom he'd just left was another note, much longer, written on a torn piece of paper:

Lawrence: Last night we came home to find a window open, and the washing up still not done. If you look at the rota, you'll notice that you have not done chores for the past two months. There's mould in the bathroom, OPEN THE WINDOW AFTER YOU SHOWER. Also you still owe us £55 for the new washing machine that YOU broke by trying to wash jeans with coins in the pockets.

Oh and don't leave bowls in the kitchen unwashed. Last night I saw *two mice!*

Thanks.

That's it I'm staying! thought Library Cat impulsively upon learning that mice inhabited the flat in plentiful numbers.

Then a new thought occurred to him. *Why do Humans over-communicate when it comes to nonsense and under-communicate when it comes to serious things? And why do they use their voices freely when it comes to nonsense, but resort to the pen and paper when it comes to reasoning?* He looked over the two angry notes… He noticed how one was signed by "Tiff" and seemed angry but also quite warm, whereas the longer one wasn't signed by anyone and referred to "us" instead of "me". This seemed to give the vague impression that it spoke for, or was trying to look like it spoke for, the feelings of an entire group. Consequently, it possessed a certain heavy-handed gravitas, and a warmongering feel. A rhetorical flexing of the muscles. It gave the impression that the "war-on-household-chores" was not equally weighted on each side, but instead much more powerfully weighted on the side of the "us", and thus aimed to intimidate Lawrence into action by suggesting he might alienate himself even further in this barren, cold, lonely, draughty upstairs part of the flat lest he fail to respond appropriately.

Yet downstairs it was all babble and fun, and the chatter stood as irrefutable proof that any one of the downstairs students could just as easily have come upstairs and told these things to Lawrence face-to-face, but chose not to because the anonymity, and reason, and rhetorical power of a good

note nails the point home further, and is served with a bonus of a side order of ostracism. Suddenly Library Cat felt lonely, as if Lawrence's peculiar isolation up here was seeping out through the bottom of his door and across the landing and into Library Cat's skin like an airborne disease. He felt sorry for having thought him a "moron". *I bet he's colder up here as well,* considered Library Cat beginning to shiver himself. Trotting down the stairs, he tried to think about Puddle Cat to cheer himself up, but her beautiful image was lost amid the clamour and cold. He went towards the front door, looked up at the lock and mewed until someone came to his aid.

"The cat wants to go out…"

"No, no, don't let him go out! Is he OK? He might get lost. Guys I think we should call Animal Protection. What if he gets hit by a car?"

Look, I'd rather just go, thought Library Cat, feeling suspicious at the Human's sudden fit of righteousness.

"I'll take him downstairs."

Library Cat felt himself being scooped up, and bounced down the great echoing stairwell of the tenement, feeling more relieved with each descending storey until he was by the front door.

"Bye bye, puss, take care!" said the student disingenuously, closing the door behind him and leaving Library Cat alone and cold once again.

❀ Recommended Reading

The House with the Green Shutters by George Douglas Brown.

❀ Food consumed

Anchovy pizza.

❀ Mood

Curious, becoming lonely.

❀ Discovery about Humans

Humans can be alienating and cowardly when it comes to speaking their mind.

The Black Dog

...in which our hero fails to recognise himself

And then some days, everything is strange.

Just over a week had passed since Library Cat's attempt to go missing. His old home returned to him in a sort of embrace with each vase and box of books seeming to apologise for having stood by silent during his untimely exodus. Nothing was said about the library books; they stood in his bedroom stacked up just as they usually did. With each afternoon that passed a heavy, grey rain lashed the windowpanes like a malevolent ghost, harder and harder as winter sunk its jaw deeper and deeper. Ginger-coloured leaves started to blacken and rot. People stopped going outside. Cats stayed in the warm.

And yet this particular day saw Library Cat on a long walk. Something was scurrying in his mind, around and around day and night, keeping him awake. A walk was always an attempt to purge such cog-spinning moods. They always seemed to help. They always seemed to ease things…

At this hour – 4 am – the drizzle had given way to a velvety, clear night. The moon hung freshly in the sky above, decorated with countless stars that flickered like lighthouses across a misty, calm sea. On the fuggy Cowgate, the moon's whiteness illuminated the backs of mice and rats as they scurried behind bins and down drains.

And yet Library Cat hardly noticed them.

As he climbed Borthwick's Close towards the Royal Mile, a particularly foolhardy rat scuttled right across his paws. Yet Library Cat hardly winced.

As the clock of St Giles chimed the hour of 4.15 am, our little black and white cat was struck with a curious feeling. It washed right over him with the same speed it takes light to travel two inches, and in its vast soundless wake, a deep and profound tiredness seemed to spread through his body and sink down into his every limb. Somewhere, deep within the plumbing of his brain, a plug had been pulled. The elixir that swirled down the plughole, sparkling and unstoppable like the sand of an egg timer, was neither the iridescent manna of happiness, nor indeed the red, clotting molasses of fear or anger or jealousy.

It was, quite simply, the elixir of *wellbeing*.

Library Cat walked the length and breadth of the Royal Mile for several hours. *It'll be gone soon, it'll be gone soon, it'll be gone soon.* Something, and he wasn't sure quite what, was getting the better of him. He skulked up past the gallant City Chambers and eerie Mercat Cross where foreign tourists had already started to congregate for the day's first underground ghost tours. Several people spotted him and came over to tickle him.

"Here, puss puss puss puss!"

But Library Cat just walked on, not even stopping to see who they were. The cobbles felt tacky under his paws; some were lathered with spilt fizzy drink, while others were thickly rinded with food muck. Normally, these might consist of little snacks. But right now, Library Cat felt he hardly even had the energy to sniff them.

It must be made clear at this point, Human, that normally Library Cat felt perfectly comfortable in his own company. He would trot along with his mind stretched out alongside the warm embers of his thoughts. He would heat his soul by them and feel them diversify his emotions. They made him feel free and alive. But now his thoughts seemed to writhe like salted slugs, their churning a physical agony, and their twisted dance too ghastly to behold. Library Cat wanted rid of them. Loneliness started to tower up around him in great sheets of Perspex. He suddenly felt enclosed within the sheets. Life felt muted. Other Humans felt distant; even their chatter and coos of affection felt as if he was hearing them down a long, hollow pipe.

But the salted slugs writhed louder than ever in a froth of red, like the macabre death cries of a bloody war that no one else could see.

What's going on?

As he turned the corner onto George IV Bridge, he noticed odd new thoughts rushing into his head that seemed to open and close absurdly like tiny little cocktail umbrellas. One such thought he had was to chase his tail, and that if he did, his mind would feel much better.

I outright refuse, thought Library Cat sternly to himself, the still-glimmering rational quarters of his brain kicking in. *I'm not going down that road again. You can give that one up, Brain.*

Library Cat had once had the misfortune to be struck down with a severe bout of tail chasing in his younger years. "Silly Cat!" the Humans would say, many of them laughing at the same time. "Probably got fleas… quit being daft!" What none of them seemed to understand was just how strangely addictive tail chasing was to the cat in question.

Aside from knocking over various ceramic ornaments, tipping them precariously towards the fireside and setting many a plate of food flying, the tail-chasing cat in question would often be scolded by a proximate Human for "being so stoooooopid". This was difficult to hear, when your brain was completely deluded and telling your paws and your mouth that your tail really was a mouse, when deep down you knew, really, something was wrong with your head but you couldn't do anything about it, because your head was in charge of you, and yet it was short-circuiting like a snake devouring its own tail.

Nope, not going down that road again, thought Library Cat with conviction.

For a moment, at least, he felt better. The warm smell of butter and croissants hit his nostrils as he sauntered past the Elephant House café. Over in the graveyard behind Greyfriars Kirk, he could see a clutch of cats, skulking between the headstones. He wondered whether going to see them might shake off his foul mood; it would be a means of distraction after all. But something about the way the cats moved and hissed at each other suggested they were not especially nice cats, and so were probably not worth the time, and might make him feel even stranger. And he was simply not in the mood for a catnip tryst.

Home. Home would surely help. A warm radiator, some food, a read, and then maybe head for a nap in the turquoise chair and a trip up to the Towsery to hang out among like-minded cats. This would surely make things better. It was okay, he was in control.

Nearly there, he thought as he saw the blocky university buildings stubbing into the grey sky above. *Focus, focus, there are many cats who are much worse off than me, I'm sure…*

But the moment Library Cat attempted to gain perspective by recalling all the other suffering in the world, a great mushroom cloud of all the global misery seem to splurge up into his mind: homeless cats, abused cats, cats maltreated by their Humans, cats living in slums, cats teased by their owners, cats with horrible life-threatening diseases… sacrificed cats. He soon began to feel ill-justified in having ever felt happiness at all, as if his suffering so paled in comparison to all the other greater sufferings on earth that his feeling unhappy was, itself, utterly indulgent, and that all the pleasures he'd derived in life so far – the reading, the strokes from Humans, the catnip, the treats, the books – were all a great sham, like the thin flaky crust atop a planet that really only conceals the simmering, churning mass of hellish mantle underneath it, ready to bubble up the moment the crust ruptures, and that to believe anything else was pure delusion.

Library Cat slowed his pace and looked down at his paws advancing on the pavement. *Left paw, Right paw, Black leg, White Leg, Left paw, Right paw, Black leg, White Leg.* New thoughts were now coming into his mind. Weird thoughts. Strange thoughts…

Am I those things?

… grey thoughts, bitter thoughts; a whole fog of putrid, multi-coloured thoughts that twisted inexorably through his brain like fairy light cabling. He turned off Middle Meadow Walk towards George Square, the nettles around its perimeters seeming to rise up and grab the air like eerie sea anemones. He had never seen them in that way before, but now felt like he couldn't see them in any other way. They frightened him. Things seemed out of focus.

And still the temptation to chase his tail…

Don't be silly, Library Cat. You know it's futile and would make things worse.

And then it was upon him. An odd smell met his nostrils, cadaverous and brown and heavy as lead. It struck Library Cat strange that a smell could be heavy and brown, but this smell was undoubtedly both these things. So nauseating was the smell that a mere wisp of it across his nostrils, disturbing the otherwise chill air, sent a deep heat into him, making him gag.

And then he saw it.

Between where he stood and the warm refuge of the library was the Black Dog. It had caught Library Cat's scent.

Library Cat felt his pupils widen and his back arch as an unspeakable terror shot through his bones. His gaze locked onto the Black Dog, snapping only right and left when he was brave enough to look for a tree to climb, or a something to bolt beneath. There was nothing. All at once the Black

Dog's head turned. In the cold air, Library Cat saw two tiny yellow eyes, as small as pinpricks, that seemed to strobe bluey-yellow like tiny fusing light bulbs. The fur was smarmed with what seemed like grease, twisting it in all directions – sometimes up in a tuft, sometimes flat along its back, and sometimes back on itself. It had no collar and Library Cat could not tell its breed. In fact it seemed difficult to suggest it had any breed in it at all, crossed or otherwise. There was something not-of-this-earth about the Black Dog.

At that moment, the Black Dog neared towards him, its back arched ready for combat. Its jowls drawled with grey saliva that bounced up and down as it panted. Directly above it, a set of drab clouds began racing over a darkening sky like nondescript items on a speeding conveyor belt. The eyes flashed wildly, bluer and more electrical as the distance between cat and dog closed. Its stench was indescribable. Finally Library Cat took a deep breath, opened his mouth, shut his eyes and let out a long sibilant hiss, as long and as loud and as threatening as he could possibly muster from his tiny cat-lungs.

And then silence. Everything except the grey clouds that scudded overhead became colourless and still. A kind of locked-in horror.

Library Cat opened his eyes. The Black Dog had fled.

Where did it go? Did I imagine it?

Ahead of Library Cat was a clear path towards the library. A car rumbled across the cobbles, and several satchelled

Humans flitted in and out of buildings. A girl came over to stroke him.

"Library Cat, there's no need to look so scared!"

The girl had blonde ringlets and weaved her fingers tenderly between his fur. She smelt sweet like oranges. Library Cat looked up at her eyes. They seemed empathetic. Despite his remoteness, Library Cat felt grateful for the company.

A little while later, he slipped away from the Human's touch and into the library.

Sleep washed over him before his head even hit his turquoise chair.

An indefinable amount of time later

Library Cat was still in his chair. It was difficult to say how long. The Black Dog had returned to him in a few sifting dreams but it hadn't lunged at him, and for this Library Cat was a little relieved. His mood was a little better; he felt rested. The mysterious chamber in his brain had magically begun refilling with the magic elixir of wellbeing. He wasn't fully restored, but he was on the mend. He still felt scared, and irritable, and jealous and angry, but that didn't matter quite so much, if the wellbeing elixir was refilling. With no wellbeing elixir these emotions were unpalatable and overwhelming like squash concentrate. When diluted in the elixir, however, they turned into little threads of colour that swept through the clear water of his mind making marvellous patterns in their myriad colours. They made up his character.

I still don't want to go outside again yet. I want to make sure the dog's gone – away from George Square, away from Edinburgh. Oh… hello Humans…

All of a sudden, a large clutch of students had gathered around Library Cat. Realising he'd spent a long time in the library and had not returned home for quite some time, they began to get worried for him. So much so, in fact, that they had even alerted something called a "Tabloid Newspaper" – a dubious compilation of Human writings – that he had run away.

Well I'm here and I'm here to stay, thought Library Cat, craning his head forward like a plank, his eyes gummed shut, purring softly. He felt touched by the concern.

Even more touching, though, was the sudden swathe of concerned correspondences Library Cat received from his cousins. Biblio Chat, for one, had risen out of his lofty contemplative remove and shown an uncharacteristic amount of concern for his Scottish cousin; said he should try thinking through these issues with another cat… *un chat thérapeutique et professionnel…* who may be able to help. Maybe the spectre of the Black Dog originated in kittenhood? Saaf Landan Tom's advice was of a rather different vein: "My cat flap's always open mate. If you need to cotch at mine, yeah? Ya wiv me, bruv, yeah? It'll pass, mate, we'll get you out on da alley again in no time."

Tom's response was brave. Library Cat had, after all, lashed out at his cousin the month before, causing him to flee, even though Tom had never meant to harm by stealing his food, and even though he could have retaliated and made short work of his black and white cousin if he'd wished. And yet Tom, with a perturbed swish of his great bushy ginger tail, and a few licks of his bloody paw, had clearly put the matter behind him, and forgiven his cousin for swiping. That took a lot. That took being the bigger cat…

Saaf Landan Tom had then suggested – meaning well, of course – that his cousin procure some of the potent catnip offered by the alley cats of Tollcross in exchange for certain "literatures". Though grateful, Library Cat was sceptical of the advice after a bad experience that once resulted in a bout of torturous rodent-based hallucinations. One could never trust the Tollcross Nip.

Library Cat thought it curious how, despite remaining sceptical about the advice offered by his cousins, he derived a definite warmth and reassurance from it nevertheless. And Saaf Landan Tom talked about feelings… Saaf Landan Tom *never* talked about feelings.

I should stop sending my cousins to Coventry, Library Cat suddenly thought, feeling a little ashamed. *What's more, if I send them to Coventry, they end up sending me to Coventry, and that defeats the point. Because we end up being in Coventry together. And surely the last place two cats would want to be, whether they get on or not, is Coventry.*

At times like this, Library Cat wondered whether it might've been easier if he hadn't been born a thinking cat – if he'd never had the warm, heady nirvana-pleasures of the Towsery, or the densely punctuated lines of Friedrich Nietzsche to send bright, happy thoughts across the pitchfork entrails of his synapses. He thought of all those cats who were not thinking cats. Right now they were all over Scotland: double-helixing their way between their Humans' legs, neck craned up at a chicken titbit; offering purrs indiscriminately to whomever stopped to stroke them; chasing bits of string entirely at the whim of Human masters; trying to scream down their own reflection in long, thin IKEA mirrors…

Would it be easier to be like them? wondered Library Cat.

But no sooner had Library Cat begun to deconstruct the question and think of it from myriad angles than more Humans arrived with strokes and tickles. One even had some bacon rind. Another spoke softly and smelt nice.

Library Cat couldn't tell how, but he was definitely feeling better. And it was down to the right company. He had never been so pleased for the affection of the student Humans.

Some three weeks earlier, in George Square, a lady and her son had been out walking their dog. The day had been beautifully clear, but now the clouds were racing and the lady worried that they may well be caught in one of those unforgiving Edinburgh downpours. As they let their dog off the lead to bound around the perimeters of the square, the young boy piped up to his mother.

"Mummy, that cat's seen Toby!"

The lady furrowed her brow and called Toby back who cooperatively linked back with his lead.

As the pair headed away from the square alongside the library towards the Meadows, the boy looked back.

"Look Mummy! Ha ha! The cat's running in circles! He's chasing his tail."

"The poor wee thing probably has fleas," the lady replied curtly, giving the dog a tug on his lead and upping her pace towards home with another suspicious glance at the sky.

❧ Recommended Reading

Reasons to Stay Alive by Matt Haig.

❧ Food consumed

Bacon rind.

❧ Mood

Empty, but improving.

❧ Discovery about Humans

They can be kind and intuitive. They can be lifesavers.

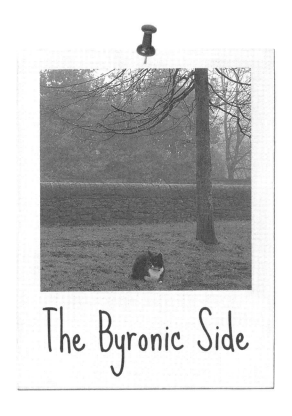

The Byronic Side

…in which our hero plays the long game

It was now two weeks until Christmas and Library Cat was feeling much better. Students were merrily singing carols, and wearing pleasingly coloured pieces of red tinsel that glittered and were most enjoyable to chase. The number of titbits also increased – turkey suddenly became plentiful as well as salmon and cream… *so much cream!* By and large, the Humans had given up their martyrish desire to keep their houses unnecessarily cold, and buildings were slowly becoming warmer, despite some of the more wealthy households remaining stubbornly and inexplicably Baltic.

The loneliness he had felt when he'd seen the Black Dog had instilled a new craving in him. He wanted a mate. A partner. Another thinking cat with whom he could share his thoughts and nuzzle against on a cold night. Puddle Cat was the one, of course. But then Puddle Cat was frustratingly enigmatic. Library Cat had spent so many hours hoping he'd see Puddle Cat again, but on the odd occasion that he did, her beautiful image would ripple into nothingness every time he attempted to drop a mouse or rat or other token of affection into her pretty mouth. It was futile.

This particular day saw Library Cat sitting on the dreich grass behind the chaplaincy. Many people seeing him might have assumed he was sitting there because the library was closed, or because the chaplaincy was being vacuumed.

They would've been wrong.

You see, Library Cat was in fact sitting out in the grey drizzle because it was time to up his game. It was 17th December (or, as we all know, the 192nd anniversary since the publication of Don Juan's 'Canto XII'), and Library Cat was attempting to channel Byron in the hope of attracting a mate. He was sure the other thinking cats in the area would get the reference. If not, they weren't worth it.

Apparently, mused Library Cat, *according to the Romantic poets, this setting of bone-numbing dampness and colour-sucking drizzle imbues me with an enigmatic quality. I am a sort of Heathcliff of cats. Thus, according to the Romantic Human masters, I will become immediately irresistible. It's a double-edged sword. I'll either receive cat love, or the Humans will think me irresistibly Romantic and lavish me with tickles.*

And so Library Cat, hunched in the cold and sporting the frown of a true method actor, waited. He waited, and waited, and waited, 'neath the symbolically spindly tree. He waited so long he forgot it was 5.55 am when he first arrived. He moved closer to the symbolically spindly tree in an effort to seem more enigmatic. He shivered. Several Humans passed by and not one cat. The Humans didn't even notice him. He shivered some more.

Am I waiting for affection, or waiting for Godot? he thought wryly to himself, temporally lifting his mood with the spark of his own Beckett-inspired wit.

Evening started to settle in, and things became silent. In the distance, he heard trains arriving at Haymarket, clicking over the tight, mirrored rails. Still no cats arrived. The odd Human raced past on a bike like a firing torpedo. Library Cat started to wonder whether there might be something else that was putting potential cats off.

Perhaps I smell strange?

Library Cat noticed how things this time of year began to smell very spicy and sugary and wondered whether she-cats were expecting him to smell the same. It seemed peculiar that they would, but then again his current strategy wasn't offering much success either. He'd tried scent marking – around the tree, and in the house, and in the library, and on his turquoise chair – but the sorry fact was that the scent mark of a thinking cat simply doesn't possess the same potency as that of an alley cat, and given thinking cats come with their own set of attractive credentials, he felt that he might as well fight the war on his terms and with his assets. "Out-think the fug", as the other Towsers would put it.

Well something has to be done, fretted Library Cat, rising slowly and shaking the dew off his fur. Books alone evidently don't cut it in the language of love. Byron was clearly a deluded cretin with some other secret trick up his sleeve that he chose not to reveal.

Poetry is a load of rubbish!

❧ Recommended Reading

'A Study of Reading Habits' by Philip Larkin.

❧ Food consumed

A bead of dew.

❧ Mood

Alluring, voluptuous.

❧ Discovery about Humans

They couldn't see a decent feline re-enactment of a Beckett classic even if it were to come up and scratch them in the face.

Sneeze

...in which our hero rolls in cinnamon

Library Cat nosed his way in through the cat flap on the hunt for a festive scent that might make him seem more attractive. The kitchen was often the place from which these smells effused so he headed there, keeping a low profile for soon there was mischief to be done. With one big leap, he was up on the kitchen work surface. Carefully he limboed under the arch of the tap spout and sidled over the gas hob. A spatula fell to the floor with a clang.

"Caaaaat?!" yelled his owner, with suspicion, from the living room.

Library Cat remained quiet. In the corner of the counter was a grassy-looking plant whose thin green stems he began to devour voraciously. Promptly afterwards he felt sick. Retching, he deposited a small soggy fur ball in the corner next to the plant and the salt and pepper shakers.

That feels better, he thought somewhat refreshed. In the other corner, he spied what he was after. He minced delicately along the counter, treading accidently on the kettle button, sending it into a furious, spitting dry boil. Finally, he sat down next to the spice rack. He biffed it with his paw. Round and round it glided, showing a blurred compound of spice names that shimmered repeatedly past his vision like a phantasmagoria or a series of atoms in a scientist's equation:

CUMIN – CINNAMON – PARSLEY – SAGE – CUMIN – CINNAMON – PARSLEY – SAGE – CUMIN – CINNAMON – PARSLEY – SAGE – CUMIN – CINNAMON – PARSLEY – SAGE

Lifting his paw, he sent the cinnamon jar flying off the merry-go-round and down to a crash on the floor.

"Caaaaaaaaaaaaaat?!"

Jumping down he sniffed and rolled in the maroon powder, until his white patches were no longer white. It smelt wonderful. This would surely give him an advantage – that stand-out-from-the-crowd edge. For who could refuse a wonderful cinnamon-scented thinking cat? He felt quite lush.

Turning round at footsteps, he saw his owner at the doorway.

"What have you done now, you wee bugger?"

Knowing this might lead to incarceration, the water spray or dried food for a week, Library Cat ran, eventually coming to a rest on the chaplaincy steps outside. He felt good – ennui appeased, fur ball purged and smelling sweet as befitted the season and his quest for love. He was ready to face the world again.

But then something curious happened. Suddenly his nose, he gasped, and let off three massive cat sneezes: "Fffffffftt! Fffftt! FFFFFFFFFTT!"

Now I should make clear at this point, Human, that sneezing for cats is very different to sneezing for us Humans. When we sneeze, we wipe our noses and move on. We realise that certain things make us sneeze, like pepper, dust, spice and pollen. But when Library Cat sneezes, he doesn't know what is happening. His world folds in on itself: he feels alarmed, possessed and out-of-control. To top it all, he feels scared.

And his response? The same as that of any other cat when faced with something alarming and inexplicable: to glare at the nearest Human, with a mixture of distain and fear, as if they are solely to blame… on this occasion, a parking attendant in the middle of George Square.

But the parking attendant merely walked by, busy issuing a fine to a man whose ticket had expired 23 seconds ago and who, at this very moment, was sprinting over the cobbles clutching a coffee yelling, "You b*****d! I was only in ****ing Sainsbury's, you ********!"

Perfectly horrendous, thought Library Cat. *Maybe it isn't the Humans that make me "Fffffft" after all.* He recalled having once before asked Biblio Chat about who was to blame for the strange "*ffffft*" phenomenon.

"Ah oui, le 'Fffffffft!'" responded Biblio Chat. "Je 'Ffffffftt' beaucoup en été! Le cause? Un mystère…"

"A mystery," thought Library Cat, disappointed. "But surely everything has a cause? A reason? A purpose? A function?"

"Non, de temps en temps, les chats – on ne sait pas toutes les réponses. On doit l'accepter, et tourner la page…"

"Sometimes we just have to accept things and move on?"

"Oui."

"Like the Human folly, and the laws of love?"

"Oui, exactement, comme la folie des humains et les lois de l'amour."

Library Cat yawned. This was far too much. Too much activity for one day. Too many null-achievements. It was time to sleep.

❧ Recommended Reading

Submarine by Joe Dunthorne.

❧ Food consumed

Cinnamon.

❧ Mood

Curious, startled.

❧ Discovery about Humans

Sometimes cats accuse them falsely.

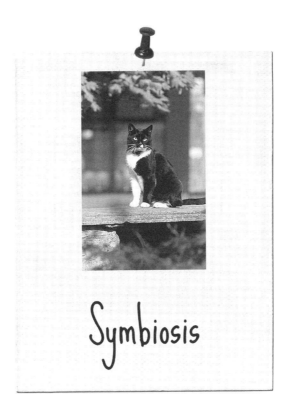

Symbiosis

...in which our hero
realises it was all in his head

The next morning, snow was falling outside and Library Cat found himself thinking about all the things he'd discovered about Humans over the last three months. He thought about how cats definitely had some things sussed like relaxing, savouring food, a respect for nature and a disinclination to stand for nonsense. But then he thought about how the

Humans had sussed things that cats hadn't, like machines that move, healthcare, buildings and how to fix roads. But then there were things that the Humans *thought* they had sussed but were actually embodiments of a kind of madness, like politics and wars and firework night and academic essay writing.

And finally there were feelings and emotions. Humans tended to conceal their emotions and hide them behind silence or equivocal language. Cats expressed their emotions viscerally on their faces and in the movement of their tails, and used written language purely for learning and enjoyment. They relished its folly, its dance of meanings and sounds. They understood its limitations. It was a shame that there was no feasible way for Human and cat to speak to each other, but then Library Cat got the overwhelming impression that Humans were sometimes so oblivious to the world around them that they were beyond learning from cats.

Maybe they like us so much because they can imbue us with their own emotions, mused Library Cat smacking his lips and washing his face. *We provide a sort of reciprocity for their feelings. At least that would explain their stupid cooing and sudden fits of sentimentality around anything with fur and four legs.*

He thought back at how contentment is the most important feeling for a cat and how undervalued it seemed at present for Humans. Instead, it was often usurped by its evil twin sister: desire. Humans thought that certain objects or people would make them suddenly happy, like chocolate or a partner with money, whereas really their discontentment rested within themselves, and these other things were a kind of smokescreen to divert their attention away from the truth – a self-deception in which they were all too adept at upholding.

But then he thought how cats and Humans were similar. Their emotions were the same, and would eternally remain so. Shame would always be shame, happiness would always be happiness, and jealousy always jealousy. They both had intelligence and he noticed how, for thinking cats at least, the two species had a choice: they could either *think* life or *live* life. Thinking life had many pleasures. Thinking was beautiful, after all. Thinking was the loveliness of Puddle Cat, the Towsery in candlelight, literature read in George Square in summer, the Enlightenment, Romanticism, Modernism, the Classics and the entire cornucopia of knowledge that adorns the colourful fruit bowl of our civilised world. But thinking could backfire. It could be frustratingly elusive and never quite reach the kernel. Worse still, it could go dangerously wrong. Despotic regimes. The slaughter of felines as devil-servants in the Middle Ages. The Black Dog… All were cases of erroneous thinking – little pieces of malware in the computer programming of the mind.

Living life was different. Living life was going hunting or On The Prowl… getting stroked or venturing on ill-advised adventures smelling of cinnamon. Living life gave you experience, and lifted you beyond your own thoughts and into the lives of others. It was palpable. Living was being *in the moment*. Saaf Landan Tom had it sussed: half thinking cat, half alley cat; half body, and half mind…

Library Cat suddenly listened to his heart. Its thump made the sound: *IAMS – IAMS – IAMS – IAMS*. (Clearly he was hungry.)

Living life is real, he rejoiced suddenly. *Real like my beating heart.*

He sniffed his food bowl and ate a big chunk of tuna. He thought about the cute tortoiseshell he'd seen out On The Prowl with Saaf Landan Tom and the wonderful few moments they had shared before she hissed. He recalled the realness of her purr and soft cheek, and how they made him feel alive and blissful. Now he thought of Puddle Cat – her glimmering fur, fine tail and deep blue smile that seemed to conceal a world of secrets. He closed his eyes. The thoughts of her spun sumptuously round in circles like toffee apples at a village fair, each one delicious but as hard to capture as the next. He sighed. They were only thoughts. He found his mind wandering back to the Humans and the disasters that befell them when they overvalued their own thoughts. Politics, wars, the Gunpowder Plot, silly "laws" about the selling of tuna…

I must seek the tortoiseshell again, he determined suddenly, surprised at his own certitude.

She was real. *I must find her.*

❧ Recommended Reading

'The Love Song of J. Alfred Prufrock' by T.S. Eliot.

❧ Food consumed

A cryogenically frozen worm in a snowball.

❧ Mood

Thoughtful, reflective.

❧ Discovery about Humans

They tend not to live in the present.

Noel

…in which our hero finds solace in Christmas

A fortnight later, Christmas had well and truly arrived. The square was empty save for the odd car that growled across the cobbles. A few days earlier had been Library Cat's birthday. He had been given a balloon by his Human with the number 9 on it and the words "Happy Birthday!!!" along the top, clearly with little concern for his globophobia.

He eyed it with suspicion as it glided disconcertingly from one room to the next, neither on the floor nor the ceiling, a big red cushion of evil, its every detail, from its alarming turgidity to its thoughtless smattering of exclamation marks, rending him tense and uncomfortable.

On the plus side, he'd been given some cream, a catnip ball and copious amounts of tickles and scratches. But then the Humans had started to run mad. One had uprooted a tree and brought it in the house and dressed it with tiny lights, while another constructed a minute barn in the hallway and started singing to a minute ceramic figurine baby. Then there were cards with a picture of the baby; pictures of the baby on the television, and people talking about the baby in hushed revered words, while televisions, radios and stereos blared music with the words "Noel, Noel, Noel, Noel. Born is the King of Israel!"

Library Cat could therefore only assume this important baby was called "Noel". He researched in the Towsery to find the reason behind this Noel's importance, but could find very few leads. The closest he came to an answer was a man called "Noel Edmonds" who was on television and presented a programme in which other Humans guessed what number was contained inside a box.

This Noel is definitely making the Humans jolly, that's for sure, thought Library Cat. *Fancy being the King of Israel.*

He ventured out into the square to let his Christmas dinner digest. He gazed over at the library. It was completely empty, the doors locked and the lights off. It seemed strange. He thought of it during term time, of its many lighted floors, stacked like buttered bread, its basement technical, its staff hierarchical, its computers layered with secret password-protected stories… And minds everywhere so deep in thought that the very act of standing up would be like unplugging a great lake.

Where are they all now?

But in spite of the silence, Library Cat felt a strange "lift". In the chaplaincy, he'd been tickled. Twice. Thrice even. He'd been given a handsome red collar which, admittedly, he'd gnawed off immediately, but he appreciated the sentiment. He'd sat on laps, chased paper around a strange interior tree and slept beside a fire. And the turkey, and the gifts of Whiskas and catnip toys from well-wishers had all been very pleasant. And merrily offered.

Yes, merriness, thought Library Cat. He felt it. And, even more surprisingly, he felt himself wishing it upon others too – other Humans, and other cats, but above all the students. He missed them.

He sat. He purred. He dozed blissfully, his tummy still full. *Yes, Merry Christmas everyone, Merry Christmas indeed!* he thought dreamily as he wended his way back to the chaplaincy to remind himself of the fate of Ebenezer Scrooge.

❧ Recommended Reading

A Christmas Carol by Charles Dickens.

❧ Food consumed

Cream.

❧ Mood

Merry (but on edge around balloon).

❧ Discovery about Humans

They can be most generous of spirit.

Library Cat's Bibliography

Brown, George Douglas, *The House with the Green Shutters* (1901)

Brown, H. Jackson, *Life's Little Instruction Book* (1991)

Carter, Angela, *Fireworks: Nine Profane Pieces* (1974)

Dickens, Charles, *A Christmas Carol in Prose, Being a Ghost-Story of Christmas* (1843)

Dunthorne, Joe, *Submarine* (2008)

Eliot, T.S., 'The Love Song of J. Alfred Prufrock', from *Prufrock and Other Observations* (1917)

Fry, Stephen, *More Fool Me* (2014)

Haig, Matt, *Reasons to Stay Alive* (2015)

Heaney, Seamus, 'Digging', from *Death of a Naturalist* (1966)

Hugo, Victor, *Les Miserables* (1862)

Joyce, James, *Ulysses* (1922)

Larkin, Philip, 'Ambulances', from *The Whitsun Weddings* (1961)

Larkin, Philip, 'A Study of Reading Habits', from *The Whitsun Weddings* (1961)

Larkin, Philip, 'Whatever Happened', from *The Less Deceived* (1955)

Lee, Harper, *To Kill a Mockingbird* (1960)

Orwell, George, *Nineteen Eighty-Four* (1949)

Pirsig, Robert M., *Zen and the Art of Motorcycle Maintenance* (1974)

Shakespeare, William, 'Sonnet 18' (1609)

Timpane, John, *Poetry for Dummies* (2001)

Welsh, Irvine, *Trainspotting* (1993)